AT PRIOR PARK

AND OTHER PAPERS

PRIOR PARK: GARDEN FRONT

(FROM A PHOTOGRAPH)

AT PRIOR PARK

AND OTHER PAPERS

BY

AUSTIN DOBSON

Ne nous servons
point de paroles
plus grandes que
les choses.

Essay Index Reprint Series

BOOKS FOR LIBRARIES PRESS
FREEPORT, NEW YORK

First Published 1925
Reprinted 1970

STANDARD BOOK NUMBER:
8369-1567-4

LIBRARY OF CONGRESS CATALOG CARD NUMBER:
73-105007

PRINTED IN THE UNITED STATES OF AMERICA

TO

SIR ALFRED BATEMAN, K.C.M.G.

MY DEAR BATEMAN,

I think you have done me the honour of reading some of these papers in their periodical form. This—in my opinion—should of itself suffice to distinguish you from those who have not made an equally commendable use of their opportunities. But I have another motive in dedicating this volume to you. For more than forty years I have enjoyed the privilege of your friendship, which is a better testimony to your powers of longsuffering than if I proffered you a certificate of heroic endurance as a student of fugitive prose.

Sincerely yours,

AUSTIN DOBSON.

CONTENTS

PAGE

At Prior Park 1

The Portraits of Carmontelle . . . 32

Garrick's 'Grand Tour' 62

Loutherbourg, R.A. 94

A Fielding 'Find' 128

The Bailli de Suffren 150

Eighteenth-Century Stowe 180

Robert Lloyd 210

Gray's Biographer 243

Appendix A (Carmontelle's Transparencies) 275

Appendix B (Exhibitions of the Eidophusikon) 277

Appendix C and Postscript (Death of the Bailli de Suffren) 282

Index 289

ILLUSTRATIONS

Prior Park: Garden Front. From a Photograph *Frontispiece*

Carmontelle. By Himself *to face page* 48

The Two Garricks. By Carmontelle *to face page* 68

Loutherbourg. From the Portrait by Gainsborough in the Dulwich Gallery *to face page* 94

The Bailli de Suffren. From the Portrait by François Gérard *to face page* 150

Princess Amelia's Arch at Stowe. From the Engraving by Thomas Medland *to face page* 202

AT PRIOR PARK

HENRY FIELDING has many memories in Bath—some definite, some doubtful; some of long standing, others of more recent discovery. One of his occasional pieces was an impromptu in the Pump Room to a shadowy 'Miss H—land'—a performance which preserves the name of that once popular physician and translator of 'Persius,' Dr. Thomas Brewster, who afterwards attended the philosopher Square; a second, entitled 'Plain Truth,' is the panegyric of another Cynthia of the minute, Miss Betty Dalston, apparently the sister of a local minor poet. At the then-secluded church of St. Mary, Charlcombe, Fielding married his first wife, Charlotte Cradock of Salisbury; from Bath, ten years later, with loving and lavish ceremonial, he brought her dead body to London for interment in the chancel vault of St. Martin's-in-the-Fields.[1] Around Bath, rather than elsewhere, cluster most of the traditions connected with the composition of his greatest novel—that master-

[1] Godden's 'Henry Fielding,' 1910, p. 153.

B

piece for which a later Bath frequenter, Mr. Samuel Richardson (the wish being father to the thought) predicted the duration of a firework. Parts of the book, it is quite possible, may have been written at Salisbury, at Twickenham, at Barnes Common, and half a dozen other places; but a large proportion was undoubtedly penned within sound of the Abbey bells; and if not at Widcombe House or Prior Park, either at the modest villa on the Avon at Twerton with the phœnix crest over the door, or at the still humbler retreat in Church Lane, now dignified into a 'Lodge,' where its author so often sought sanctuary with his sister Sarah. From the 'little parlour' at Yew Cottage, as it was then called, if anywhere, must have issued that proud invocation to Fame at the beginning of Book Thirteen—an invocation which, it may be observed, has enjoyed the exceptional advantage of being heard. But of all the associations that connect Fielding with the 'Queen of the West,' there is none more ancient and less uncertain than that which links him with Ralph Allen, the 'Squire Allworthy' of 'Tom Jones.'

As it is with Allen's residence and friends rather than with Allen and his biography, that we are for the present concerned, it can hardly be needful to deal at length with the oft-told story of the circumstances which raised him from obscurity to opulence. But, remembering the useful caveat of Pope that

> Men must be taught as if you taught them not,
> And things unknown propos'd as things forgot,

no great harm can be done by 'reminding' the reader briefly of the leading facts of his career. Ralph Allen was the son of the landlord of the 'Duke William' or 'Old Duke' Inn at St. Blazey in Cornwall. His grandmother kept the post-office at St. Columb, not many miles away; and being employed here as a boy, his alertness and intelligence attracted the notice of the district surveyor, in consequence of which he was transferred to the Bath Post Office. He had inborn gifts for organisation; and his foot once on the ladder, his ascent was assured. The timely discovery of a projected English rising in connection with Mar's rebellion, procured him at once the favour of the Ministry; the patronage of General (afterwards Marshal) Wade, then stationed at Bath; and, in due course, the office of Bath Post-master. In this capacity he set about the much-needed task of reforming the very rudimentary postal service. In those days, the days of the first George, except over certain radial routes to and from the capitals of the three kingdoms, there was practically no transmission of mails, and bye or lateral communication between county and county or town and town, was of the most dilatory and circuitous description. Although a Post Office Act of 1711 had afforded scope for what are known as 'cross-posts,' nothing much had been done.[1] Nine years later, Allen, being then no more than six and twenty, took up the work. He obtained a concession from the Government empowering him to establish better methods, and virtually to re-arrange, in these respects, the entire letter-carrying machinery of England and Wales. For this he had to pay a heavy annual 'consideration'; and his first essays were necessarily made at a loss. But in the end his energy and resource triumphed over every obstacle; and although, on subsequent renewal of the contract, the rent was raised, his profits by degrees became so considerable as to make him a rich man. By the simultaneous exploitation of

[1] 'A *bye* or *way* letter would be a letter passing between any two towns on the Bath Road and stopping short of London—as, for instance, between Bath and Hungerford, between Hungerford and Newbury, between Newbury and Reading, and so on; while a *cross-post* letter would be a letter crossing from the Bath Road to some other—as, for instance, a letter between Bath and Oxford.' (Joyce's 'History of the Post Office,' 1893, p. 147.)

the valuable oolite quarries at Hampton and Combe Downs near Bath, he not only materially increased his already ample means, but added to the architectural beauty of the town, while his generous use of his wealth earned him the merited reputation of a public benefactor. He died in June 1764, aged seventy-one, and is buried under a beautiful mausoleum in Claverton churchyard. He was twice married, his second wife, Elizabeth Holder, surviving him. A monument was erected to him on a part of his estate, which is also a monument to the bad taste of his heir, Bishop Warburton.

With the historical 'Bath stone' of the re-opened quarries at Combe and Hampton Downs is also connected that famous mansion which must always be remembered with Ralph Allen's name. For many years his town residence had been a house to the rear of York Street in Lilliput Alley (now part of North Parade Passage);[1]

[1] In Lilliput Alley, the Lilliputian historian delights to remark, once lived the celebrated Sally Lun of the tea-cake and the ballad-mongers:

> 'No more I heed the muffin's zest,
> The Yorkshire cake or bun;
> Sweet Muse of Pastry! teach me how
> To make a "Sally Lun."'

but in later life he migrated to Prior Park, a house he had built on Widcombe Hill, a little to the south-east of Bath, and commanding through a hollow a fine view of the city, four hundred feet below. Its origin was on this wise. Bath stone was beginning to be used freely, not only for facings and ornamentation, but for building;[1] and gradually what is now known as modern Bath was slowly coming into shape and being. Queen Square, begun in 1728, was finished in 1735, in which latter year the North and South Parades were also completed. But Bath stone had a formidable competitor in Portland stone, and bitter enemies in the London architects, who contemptuously compared it, both for colour and durability, to Cheshire cheese. All these prejudices Allen's patience had to overcome, not without difficulty; and he resolved to give the adversary an object-lesson in the matter by building, in the neighbourhood of his Combe Down works, a

[1] The house in St. John's Place now known as the Garrick's Head, and once inhabited by Richard Nash, was one of the earliest examples of Bath Stone decoration. Mrs. Delany and Miss Berry afterwards lived in it. There is a good representation of it in J. F. Meehan's interesting 'Famous Houses of Bath, etc.,' 1901, 41—a work in which, following the precept of Linnaeus, the author has worthily commemorated his locality.

sumptuous mansion of Bath stone, which should not only exhibit the superlative quality of the maligned material both for ornamentation and construction, but illustrate and exemplify the 'Orders of Architecture in all their glory.' Modified, as might be expected, by after-considerations, and less ambitious in the execution than in the conception, Prior Park was begun about 1735. Its erection completely vindicated the capabilities of oolite; while the concurrent construction of the General, or Mineral Water Hospital (1738-42), to which Allen, besides a donation of £1,000, presented all the necessary stonework, certainly did not diminish the prestige of the proprietor of the quarries.

John Wood, the architect, and first of the name, who, it should also be stated, gave his professional services to the Hospital gratis, describes Prior Park as consisting of 'a Mansion House in the center, two Pavilions, and two Wings of Offices. All these are united by low buildings, and while the chief Part of the whole Line fronts the Body of the City, the rest faces the summit of *Mar's Hill*,' namely—Mount Beacon, or Lansdown. The first part of this short description suggests a superficial affinity to Stowe,[1] and pro-

[1] See *post*, 'Eighteenth-Century Stowe.'

bably to other eighteenth-century country-seats. The central structure, in the Corinthian style on a rustic basement, occupied 150 out of the 1200 feet of the frontage, and rose from a terrace 100 feet below the summit of Combe Down. The entrance was in the south front; on the north front, or garden side, stood a stately six-column portico, intended by its designer to rival and even excel that erected for Sir Richard Child, at Wanstead House in Essex, by Campbell of Greenwich Hospital, one of the most determined detractors of Bath Stone. Between its Ionic pillars were balustrades converting the whole into an alfresco pavilion from which it was possible at once to enjoy the air and the magnificent view of distant Bath.[1] Below the terrace on which the house was built, the ground sloped gradually in lawn and garden beds; while a spring from the summit, falling by careful lapses and contrived cascades, found its way at last into a lake, well stocked with fish, about a quarter of a mile distant. At the head of this lake there was, as at Stowe, a Palladian Bridge, a copy by Richard Jones, Allen's factotum and clerk of the works, of that erected by Lord Pembroke at Wilton in Wiltshire. Jones was also responsible for the west wing of the

[1] See the frontispiece to this volume.

house which was finished after Allen had dispensed with the services of his original architect Wood, who died in 1754. To complete the resemblance to Stowe, it may be added that, in 1752, soon after the erection of the Palladian Bridge, Prior Park was visited by the Princess Amelia; and Allen, retiring himself to another seat he had at Weymouth, surrendered the house to his illustrious guest. But there is no record that he erected a Doric Arch in Her Royal Highness's honour; nor on this occasion had she any Walpole in her suite to play Polonius, and chronicle her diversions.

Prior Park, apparently, was not like Stowe, a treasure-house of works of art, or even a museum of curiosities. But it is nearly as memorable by its visitors, some of whom, for example—Pitt and Pope, were common to both places. The first-comer, in point of time, as well as in prominence, was Pope. Pope's relations with Allen were, however, more creditable to the host than the guest; and they constitute one of the more equivocal chapters of Pope's equivocal biography. They cover the last eight years of his life; and arose out of the issue, from 'Curll's chaste press,' of his so-called spurious or pirated correspondence. With this, it will be remembered, Pope professed to be indignant, although in reality he was an accessary. Allen, one of whose most engaging qualities, in addition to simplicity, seems to have been a genuine veneration for goodness, was struck by the highly edifying sentiments which the letters expressed; and in order to ensure their reproduction in authentic form, wrote to Pope offering to pay the cost of a new edition. Pope replied with polite ambiguity, promising to avail himself of Allen's proposal, should it become necessary. Thereupon Allen busied himself actively in soliciting subscriptions to the folio and quarto issues of 1737. His advocacy was very genuine and effective, and indeed there is every reason to believe that, as suggested by the poet himself in one of his unpublished letters to Allen now in the British Museum,[1] his enthusiasm supplied rather more of the subscriptions than are assigned to his name. In any case, this marks the beginning of the friendship between the Man of Bath and the 'Twit'nam Bard.' Pope, who was a pioneer in the matter of landscape gardening, went on to advise Allen in the laying-out of Prior

[1] Quotations from these letters (E.C. 1947), which extend from 1736 to 1744, were made, for the first time, in vol. ii. of 'George Paston's' 'Mr. Pope: His Life and Times,' 1909.

Park, then in progress; and Allen in return contributed curious incrustations and perforated stones from the Combe Down quarries to that famous grotto by the Thames which was the plaything of Pope's declining days. Pope sent Surrey pine-apples, and Allen replied with Somerset waters. In 1738 Allen formally visited Pope at Twickenham; and the November of the following year found the poet domiciled at Prior Park, rhetorically rejoicing over his remoteness both from the Babel of London and that other mimic Babel of Bath, which he was enabled to survey, in the true Lucretian fashion, from Allen's specular portico. He must have enjoyed himself immensely, for Allen and his wife were models of considerate hospitality. On all matters horticultural Pope's word was law: and Pope had an entertainer who was also only too willing to participate in any philanthropic proposal. One of those for whom he secured Allen's assistance was the unsatisfactory Richard Savage, whom his long-suffering friends were endeavouring to establish in Wales; and the Museum correspondence shows pretty clearly that half Pope's contribution of twenty pounds for this purpose was quietly furnished by Allen's munificence. To this unobtrusive quality we owe Pope's notorious reference to his host in the dialogue which afterwards became the first 'Epilogue to the Satires:'

> Let low-born ALLEN, with an awkward shame,
> Do good by stealth, and blush to find it fame.

Allen's private views of this couplet are not on record. But, despite the admirable and antithetic dexterity of the second line, he must have been curiously constituted if he did not regard the epithet 'low-born' as even more unhappy than that of 'our little bard' which Johnson applied to Goldsmith in the first version of the Prologue to the 'Good Natur'd Man;' and though Pope, perhaps with some 'awkward shame' of his own, afterwards changed 'low-born' to 'humble,' it is difficult to believe that Allen can ever have been extravagantly gratified. But though he was not a highly educated man, he had instinctively acquired that virtue of reticence which, in such junctures, the true philosopher exhibits or simulates. He preserved a discreet silence, only redoubling, if possible, his good offices to his tactless panegyrist.

When Pope first went to Prior Park, his main regret, he told 'blameless Bethel,' had been the absence of his favourite, Martha Blount. In April 1743, that lady lost her mother, and August at last found them together at Prior Park. But the joint visit was not a success. Some obscure disagreement took place almost immediately between Mrs. Allen and Miss Blount which hurried Pope precipitately to Lord Bathurst's, and brought about a breach which, on Pope's side, was never wholly repaired. It is but just to say that Miss Blount was evidently in poor health; and that, in addition to her recent bereavement, she had vexatious domestic difficulties. The origin of the rupture has never been definitely ascertained. Whether, from the beginning, Mrs. Allen was prejudiced against her feminine guest; whether Miss Blount was more than ordinarily untunable and exacting;[1] or whether the suggested proximate cause was the refusal of Allen, who had just been Mayor of Bath, to lend the fair Patty his coach to carry her to Mass, will now probably never be known. What seems certain is—that matters had become perilously

[1] In any case, she must always have been a somewhat difficult guest. In a letter written from Stowe by Lady Suffolk in September 1735, she says that Lord Cobham had been put to much inconvenience owing to Miss Blount's reception at Stowe of friends of hers who, though neighbours, were not on his visiting list. ('Suffolk Corr.,' 1824, ii. 143.)

strained. Pope, quitting Prior Park in a crisis of nervous irritation, had left his lady friend to follow as she could. However well he might wish his host, Mrs. Allen had suddenly become 'an impertinent minx'; and Warburton, who was implicated, 'a sneaking parson.' It was Warburton, nevertheless, who, later, effected a reconciliation; and between Pope and the Allens, at all events, the old cordiality appeared to be renewed. A few months afterwards Pope died; but though by the will which he executed in December 1743, he left Allen part of his library and £150, the manner of the money bequest still betrays a residue of rancour. The sum named, said the testator, was, to the best of his calculation, what he had received from Allen, partly for his own, and partly for charitable uses. Allen promptly handed over the money to the Mineral Water Hospital (as indeed Pope had suggested) merely remarking laconically that his friend was always a bad accountant; and that a cipher added to the figures would have more accurately represented the amount of the obligation.[1] He also took into

[1] The Warburton truce took place in September 1743, and the will is dated 12th December following. It was conjectured, perhaps not unnaturally, that Miss Blount was at the bottom of the stroke at Allen; but the lady

his service Pope's faithful gardener, John Searle, who had been adequately, but perhaps not liberally, provided for by his late master. Pope had left him £100 and a year's wages. Allen gave him a second hundred and a home.

Of Warburton, already mentioned more than once, it is now time to speak. At the date of Pope's death he had been some two years an habitué of Prior Park, for admission to which he was indebted to Pope. In 1741 he was a middle-aged Lincolnshire clergyman of no great eminence, although he had already published the first part of his famous contribution to the Deistic controversy, the 'Divine Legation of Moses.' But his championship of the 'Essay on Man' against those who questioned its orthodoxy, had strongly endeared him to Pope; and when, in the year last mentioned, his proposal to visit Pope at Twickenham reached the poet at Widcombe, Pope, then wrestling with the new 'Dunciad,' eagerly availed himself of Allen's polite proposal that Warburton should join them. 'The worthy man who is the master of it [Prior Park],' he wrote enthusiastically to Warburton, 'invites you

denied this to Spence. She asserted on the contrary that she had vainly endeavoured to procure its withdrawal ('Anecdotes, etc.,' 1820, p. 357).

in the strongest terms; and is one who would treat you with love and veneration, rather than what the world calls civility and regard. He is sincere and plainer than almost any man now in this world, "antiquis moribus." . . . It is just the best season. . . . You will want no servant here. Your room will be next to mine, and one man will serve us.' And then follows a passage on the amenities of Prior Park. 'Here is a library and a gallery ninety feet long to walk in, and a coach whenever you would take the air with me.'[1] (Allen himself, it may be noted, seldom used a coach unless he went beyond Bath.) The invitation thus given was the making of Warburton. He became a regular visitor to Prior Park, preached in its chapel,[2] ingratiated himself with its open-handed proprietor, contrived to obtain the hand of Miss Gertrude Tucker, Allen's favourite niece, and eventually, through his new friend's influence with Pitt, then Member for

[1] Pope's 'Correspondence,' by Elwin and Courthope, iv. (1886), pp. 220, 221.

[2] In November 1745, he preached there a sermon 'occasioned by the present unnatural rebellion,' which was printed. The large folio Bible used in Prior Park Chapel, it may be added, was that presented to Pope by Atterbury at their last interview in the Tower. (Hill's Johnson's 'Lives of the Poets,' iii. (1905), p. 141.)

Bath, proceeded Dean of Bristol and Bishop of Gloucester. From this time forward, he virtually resided at Prior Park; and when Allen died, Warburton and his wife came in for £5,000 each, with reversion, on Mrs. Allen's death, of the Widcombe and Claverton estates.

Warburton, for all his good fortune, can scarcely be described as a very attractive personality. He evidently could be, whenever he chose, exceedingly conciliatory and agreeable; he could also be, and he frequently was, in controversy especially, insufferably rough, overbearing and abusive. Prosperous externally, it is not impossible that his prosperity had its drawbacks. His married life, according to his biographers, was not idyllic; and even when he first made Allen's acquaintance, he must have had premonitions of that ill-health which finally, like Swift's, landed him in senile decay. At Prior Park he doubtless exhibited both aspects of his disposition. To Allen, whom he genuinely respected, and to whom he was bound by the strongest ties of gratitude, he was uniformly deferential and amiable. He regarded him, he says in one of his letters, as 'the greatest character in any age of the world. . . . Charity is but a small part of his virtues. I have studied his character even maliciously, to find out where the weakness lies. But I have studied in vain.' Even a large deduction for partiality would still leave this laudation. And he proved the sincerity of his devotion by defending his benefactor strenuously when he was attacked. On the other hand, it is quite likely that to those who had less claim on him he was offensively patronizing and arrogant; and it is consoling to think that he sometimes met his match. Quin, the actor, for example, who was by no means inclined to be suppressed by the 'saucy priest,' and who had, moreover, an inconvenient habit of blunt repartee before which Warburton's erudition was powerless, sometimes effectively routed him. Once, when they were discussing the execution of Charles I, which Quin upheld, Warburton asked loftily by what law he was condemned, and Quin retorted: 'By all the law which he had left in the land!' The Bishop could find no rejoinder. On another occasion when Warburton sought to accentuate Quin's calling by insidiously asking him to recite something, Quin, yielding to pressure, selected a speech of Pierre in Otway's 'Venice Preserv'd,' containing the passage:

> *Honest men*
> Are the soft, easy cushions on which *knaves*
> Repose and fatten—

'mouthing out his hollow oes and aes' with such unmistakable application to Allen and Warburton that the latter never again troubled him for a taste of his quality as an elocutionist.[1]

Quin and Warburton were antipathetic; and it is known that some of the severer strokes in Churchill's merciless castigation of the Bishop in 'The Duellist' are based on the bons mots of the actor. But Warburton and Quin have broken our chronological sequence, as the next important of Allen's guests is undoubtedly Fielding, on whose relations with Pope and Allen the unpublished correspondence in the British Museum throws a fresh light—a light which justifies us in drawing out those relations rather more minutely than hitherto. Pope's earlier connection with Fielding is obscure. In one of Fielding's love-verses to Charlotte Cradock, he speaks of the poet as 'sweet *Pope*,' which proves nothing. Pope commented on a passage in 'Tom Thumb'; and Fielding referred obliquely to Pope in the 'Covent Garden Tragedy.' When 'Pasquin' appeared in April 1736 Pope was one of the audience—according to the 'Grub Street Journal.' But the security is no better than Bardolph's; and the statement besides was promptly contradicted.

[1] John Taylor, 'Records of my Life,' 1832, i, 86.

Four years later the 'Champion' was praising Pope's 'Iliad,' which the writer of the paper (apparently to meet the allegations of the enemy that Pope was ignorant of Greek) declared, in emphatic typography, he had, 'with *no Disadvantage to the Translator*, *COMPARED with the Original*.' In February 1742, appeared 'Joseph Andrews,' Book III, chap. vi, of which brings in both Pope and Allen: 'Some gentlemen of our cloth' [*i.e.* 'skips' or footmen], says Joseph, 'report charitable actions done by their lords and masters; and I have heard Squire Pope, the great poet, at my lady's table, tell stories of a man that lived at a place called Ross, and another at the Bath, one Al—— Al—— I forget his name, but it is in the book of verses [Pope's "Satires"]. This gentleman hath built up a stately house too, which the squire likes very well; but his charity is seen farther than his house, though it stands on a hill, ay, and brings him more honour too. It was his charity that put him in the book, where the squire says he puts all those who deserve it; and to be sure, as he lives among all the great people, if there were any such, he would know them.'

This, to all appearance, is the first mention of Allen by Fielding; and it suggests that Fielding had heard of Allen's benevolence from Pope. In a subsequent letter from Pope to Allen there is, however, a specific reference to Fielding. 'Fielding has sent the Books you subscribed for by the Hand I employed in conveying the £20 to him. In one chapter of the second vol. he has paid you a pretty Compliment upon your House.' At first sight this might seem to relate to the foregoing passage from 'Joseph Andrews,' which speaks both of Allen and his dwelling-place. But Pope's letter is dated 12th April, 1743, more than a year after the issue of Fielding's first novel, which besides was not subscribed for, but had been sold outright to Andrew Millar. The reference is therefore to the 'Miscellanies,' which were issued in April 1743; and the 'compliment' occurs at p. 42 of the second volume of these, in chap. v of the Lucianic 'Journey from this World to the Next,' etc. Contrasting the many 'noble Palaces' on the road to *Greatness*, with the absence of them on the road to *Goodness*, Fielding remarks that in the latter thoroughfare there was 'scarce a handsome Building, save one greatly resembling a certain House by the *Bath*.' This is clearly the passage indicated by Pope, who himself receives a tribute further on in chap. viii, p. 64, where Homer is said 'to have asked much after Mr. *Pope*, and said he was very desirous of seeing him: for that he had read his 'Iliad' in his Translation with almost as much delight, as he believed he had given others in the Original.' The same chapter contains a reference to Warburton.

To what extent these citations imply direct intercourse between Allen and Fielding is doubtful; and it is notable that neither Allen nor Pope appears in the list of subscribers to the 'Miscellanies.' It may be that the story of the £20—with an additional cipher!—is the source of Derrick's statement that Allen sent Fielding a present of £200 'before he personally knew him,' for Derrick, who blunders badly in another part of this very passage, cannot be regarded as very trustworthy.[1] But Fielding, whatever may have happened previous to the publication of the 'Miscellanies' in 1743, was at Bath in 1744, since, as we now know, his wife died there in November of that year; and in the interval which elapsed before the issue of 'Tom Jones' in February 1749, a period of unusual stress, ill-health and privation, he must often have visited Bath. It is admitted that he lived for some time in the house at Twerton, already referred to;[2]

[1] 'Letters,' 1767, vol. ii, 94.

[2] This, now known as 'Fielding Lodge,' is authentic-

and that while there he was writing 'Tom Jones' and dining 'almost daily at Prior Park.' So says the Rev. Richard Graves, the author, later, of that clever book, the 'Spiritual Quixote'; and he is a credible witness. Other places in Bath associated with the progress of the book are Widcombe House, the home of Allen's connections, the Bennets, with whom Fielding's acquaintance seems to go back to the time of his courtship; and he must have often resided with his sister Sarah in her little cottage in Church Lane, now transformed into Widcombe Lodge, and tableted as a site he once haunted. During all this time it is clear that he was in frequent communication with Allen; and that he was indebted to him for repeated kindnesses, which he, on his side, acknowledged with all the ungrudging gratitude which was part of his large and impulsive nature.[1]

ated by an inscription placed on it by the good offices of Mr. R. G. Naish of Twerton.

[1] Fielding's original agreement with Andrew Millar for the coyyright of 'Tom Jones, and his autograph receipt for £600, were sold at Sotheby's in June 1911 for £1,015, the late Mr. Huth having paid Sotheran £12 12*s.* for them in 1868. The author's entire gain for the six volumes was £700, as Millar afterwards added £100, in view of the success of the book.

It is true that 'Tom Jones' is inscribed not to Allen but to George Lyttelton; and that, by Fielding's dedicatory Preface, a third patron, the Duke of Bedford, is associated with the triple 'picture of a truly benevolent Mind' after which, in drawing the Allworthy of the novel, he had been endeavouring. From Bedford and Lyttelton he had certainly received pecuniary help; indeed, he not only indicates Lyttelton as the sole begetter of the book, but expressly declares that he (Fielding) 'partly owed his Existence to him' during much of the time occupied in its composition. 'Tom Jones' is nevertheless full of references to Allen, and if the book does not precisely depict Prior Park, it is from its terrace that Allworthy surveys the sunrise; and the leading traits of Allworthy are the leading traits of Allen. Kindliness, simplicity, modesty, unpretentious generosity—these are all the merits of Allworthy, and they are also the merits of Allen. Sometimes the description is literally transferable. The following, for instance, is quite unsuited to Bedford and Lyttelton, while it is exactly true of Allen: 'Though he had missed the advantage of a learned education, yet being blessed with vast natural abilities, he had so well profited by a vigorous, though late application to letters, and by much conversation with men of eminence in this way, that he was himself a very competent judge in most kinds of literature.'[1] Moreover, in Book VIII, chap. i, Fielding, though without naming Allen, draws his character at full. It is too lengthy to quote; and we have only room for a passage borrowed from an earlier page, which throws a light on the unconventional hospitalities of Prior Park. After referring to those hosts to whom their literary guests are little more than dependents, or servants out of livery, the author goes on: 'On the contrary, every person in this house was perfect master of his own time; and as he might at his pleasure satisfy all his appetites within the restrictions only of law, virtue, and religion; so he might, if his health required, or his inclination prompted him to temperance, or even to abstinence, absent himself from any meals, or retire from them whenever he was so disposed, without even a solicitation to the contrary: for indeed, such solicitations from superiors always savour very strongly of commands. But here all were free from such impertinence, not only those, whose company is in all other places esteemed a favour from their equality of fortune, but even those whose indigent circumstances

[1] 'Tom Jones,' Book I, chap. x.

make such an eleemosynary abode convenient to them, and who are therefore less welcome to a great man's table because they are most in need of it.'[1]

Fielding when at Bath continued to frequent Prior Park,[2] and he had not exhausted his gratitude to 'Mr. Allworthy,' to whom, two years later, he inscribed 'Amelia.' We have always regarded this tribute as a model of the dignified style in dedication. Here, in their first fashion, are the portions which relate to Allen: 'The best Man is the properest Patron of such an attempt. This, I believe, will be readily granted; nor will the public Voice, I think, be more

[1] 'Tom Jones,' Book I, chap. x.

[2] There is token of this in the censorious utterance of Hurd to Balguy in 1751, in which he speaks of having dined there on the previous day [18th March] with Fielding, whom he characterizes as 'a poor emaciated, worn-out rake, whose gout and infirmities have got the better even of his buffoonery.' Warburton's servile biographer, then a young man, had apparently not yet acquired the charity which later made him the admiration of Bathonians. In March 1751, Fielding had, not long before, been dangerously ill; and if he was a martyr to gout, so was Pitt. Moreover, at this date he was an active and energetic magistrate, whose philanthropic pamphlets were by no means 'buffoonery,' and whose latest novel was 'Tom Jones.'

divided, to whom they shall give that Appellation. Should a Letter indeed be thus inscribed, DETUR OPTIMO, there are few Persons who would think it wanted any other Direction.'

After saying that he will not 'assume the fulsome Stile of a common Dedicator,' he goes on: 'I have not their usual Design in this Epistle nor will I borrow their Language. Long, very long may it be before a most dreadful Circumstance shall make it possible for any Pen to draw a just and true Character of yourself, without incurring a Suspicion of Flattery in the Bosoms of the Malignant. This Task, therefore, I shall defer till that Day (if I should be so unfortunate as ever to see it) when every good Man shall pay a Tear for the Satisfaction of his Curiosity; a day which at present, I believe, there is but one good Man in the World who can think of with Unconcern.'

Notwithstanding that the owner of Prior Park was an older man than Fielding, the 'just and true Character' was never composed, for Ralph Allen survived the novelist some ten years. But he extended his benevolent protection to Fielding's family, one of whom was named Allen after him; and although he resigned the execution and administration of Fielding's will, he is said to have made a 'very liberal annual donation' towards the education of his children—a statement supported by the fact that he left three of them, as well as their aunt, Sarah, £100 each.

Fielding had been dead three years, and Pope thirteen, before we hear of the next great visitor to Prior Park, William Pitt, later Earl of Chatham. Allen had no doubt made Pitt's acquaintance before 1757, when he became Member for Bath; and their friendship continued until Allen's death. Whether, as there is some ground for supposing, Allen actually paid Pitt's election expenses or whether he did not, there can be little doubt that Allen's local influence, and power with the civic authorities, materially contributed to Pitt's success; and that the relations of the two men were honourable to both. Unluckily, towards the close of Allen's life, those relations were troubled by a passing disagreement between the Great Commoner and his constituents. Pitt regarded the Peace of Paris, which closed the Seven Years' War, as 'inadequate,' and he had said so in Parliament. When he was subsequently invited to present to the King an address from the Mayor and Corporation of Bath in which it was qualified as 'adequate,' he naturally declined to do so; and as Allen honestly admitted his responsibility for the peccant epithet, the situation became embarrassing. Between Pitt and Allen, however, matters were happily smoothed over without loss of self-respect on either side.[1] At Allen's death he left Pitt £1,000 as 'a last instance of his friendship and grateful regard for the best of friends, as well as the most upright and ablest of Ministers that has adorned our Country.' Pitt, on his side, wrote to Allen's widow of her dead husband in terms of the warmest affection and esteem. But of his actual visits to Allen's house no record remains. There was no pious poet to sing of Pitt at Prior Park as Thomson sang of Pitt at Stowe.

Pope, Fielding, Pitt—these are the most substantial shadows of the Prior Park guests; of the others we get little more than passing glimpses. Of Warburton, Graves, Quin, Hurd, and even Sarah Fielding, the most has been said that is known. There seems to be an impression that Sterne was one of the visitors. But the picture of him painted by Gainsborough, another of Allen's friends, and now in the Peel Park Museum at Salford, was not executed until after Allen's death. Of Richardson, who is also said to have sat to Gainsborough, and who married the sister

[1] Peach, 'Life and Times of Ralph Allen,' 1895, pp. 176-9.

of James Leake, the bookseller whose back-parlour on the Walks by Lilliput Alley was a rallying-place of the Bath literati, there is a solitary and very characteristic anecdote. It is here that he is recorded to have uttered the memorable words: 'Twenty years ago I was the most obscure man in Great Britain, and now I am admitted to the company of the first characters in the Kingdom.' He was going to dine at Prior Park![1] Thomas Edwards, of the 'Canons of Criticism,' Richardson's friend and admirer, and a Greek scholar bold enough to cross swords with Warburton, was another of the group; so also was that most dapper of Dukes, the French envoy, Nivernais, wearing no doubt on his extremely diminutive person the extremely diminutive hat which he had brought into fashion, and which Anstey in the 'New Bath Guide' celebrated as the mark of a 'Beau Garçon.' Other names might be added. But the pleasantest figures to pause upon are those of the host and hostess, as drawn by Derrick, one of Nash's successors as Master of the Ceremonies. Allen he portrays as 'a very grave, well-looking old man, plain in his dress, resembling that of a Quaker, and courteous in his behaviour. . . . His wife is low [*i.e.*, of stature], with grey hair, of a

[1] Graves, 'The Triflers,' 1806, p. 68.

very pleasing address, that prejudices you much in her favour.'[1] One wants no fuller picture of that homely, kindly pair; but those who desire further to visualize 'Mr. Allworthy' may consult William Hoare's picture in that Hospital at Bath to which Allen was so munificent a patron.

[1] 'Letters,' 1767, ii, 94.

THE PORTRAITS OF CARMONTELLE

AT Strawberry-Hill, in the sunny Blue Breakfast Room overlooking the Thames with its solemn, slow-moving barges, hung many mementoes of Horace Walpole's friends and predilections. There were prints of Lady Mary Coke, Lady Hervey, and Mason the poet; there was a sketch of Fontenelle; there was a portrait of Voltaire cut out in card by Hubert of Geneva. There was a painting by Raguenet of the Hôtel de Carnavalet 'in la rue Coulture St. Catherine, at Paris,' now an Historical Museum, but once the residence of Mme. de Sévigné; and there was an engraving minutely reproducing Mme. du Deffand's room and her favourite cats, a taste in which she rivalled her contemporary, Mme. Helvétius. But the picture that here most immediately concerns us was a washed drawing in which a young, aristocratic-looking woman, in the 'robe rayée' of the period, was shown presenting a doll to an old lady in a frilled hood-cap, who, seated in a high chair, and with closed eyes, was raising her hands to receive it.

The figures stood for two of Walpole's French friends, the Duchesse de Choiseul, the young and beautiful wife of Louis the Fifteenth's Prime Minister, and Mme. du Deffand, then more than seventy years old. Mme. du Deffand had long been blind; but was still possessed of extraordinary vivacity and feverish interest in life. Her own grandmother had been a Duchesse de Choiseul; and in allusion to this, she was accustomed to call the existing Duchess 'Grand'maman,' while that lady on her side addressed her septuagenarian friend as her 'petite-fille.' Hence, apparently, what Walpole styles the 'joli badinage de la poupée.' Not long after his second visit to Paris, the two ladies had sent him their combined portraits by the hands of the French Ambassador, the Marquis du Châtelet. That of the elder lady was held to be excellent. Nothing could be so 'exactement vrai au pied de la lettre.' 'Vous êtes ici en personne, je vous parle, et il n'y manque que votre impatience ǎ répondre'—says Horace in his English-French. Her 'Tonneau' (this was her so-called 'Tub' or great chair), her furniture, her environment, were all faithfully given. 'Jamais une idée ne s'est si bien rendue.' On the other hand, the portrait of Mme. de Choiseul, whom Walpole professed to admire extravagantly, was reckoned a failure. That 'queen of an allegory,' as he called her, had lost her beauty and distinction; and probably a good deal which, in those days, when expression played so large a part in personal charm, could not possibly be transferred to paper or canvas. Even if the artist had succeeded, as he had with Mme. du Deffand—who, by the way, was practically 'still life'—something, as Walpole admits, must always have been to seek. 'L'éloquence, l'élégance, la saine raison, la bonté, l'humilité, et l'affabilité, sont-elles du ressort de la peinture?' he asks. In all this, there is no doubt a good deal of the hyperbole of compliment. But others, as well as Walpole, appear to have agreed that the popular artist, M. de Carmontelle, had not been as fortunate in his likeness of Mme. de Choiseul as in his likeness of Mme. du Deffand.[1] And who was M. de Carmontelle? That is the question we shall attempt to answer.

[1] We have failed to discover what has become of this drawing. At the Strawberry-Hill sale it was sold for seven guineas to Mr. W. M. Smith (Strawberry-Hill Cat., 1842, p. 121). An engraving of it by W. Greatbach forms the frontispiece to vol. vii. of Walpole's 'Letters' by Cunningham, 1857-59.

There seems, at the outset, to be some doubt as to the spelling of his name. Most of the dictionaries call him Carmontelle; he is Carmontelle to Grimm, whose portrait he drew; and he is Carmontelle on some of the engravings after his designs. He is also (and this is, perhaps, most to the point) Carmontelle in the official record of his death. But Walpole, Miss Mary Berry, Mme. du Deffand, and Mme. de Genlis, the last of whom says she had known him uninterruptedly for fifteen years at Paris or at the Orléans court of Villers-Cotterets, all call him 'Carmontel.' In either case, the name was assumed. The late M. Auguste Jal, of whom one may truly say, as Johnson said of Cave, that he was 'nullis fessus laboribus,' discovered conclusively that the patronymic of Carmontelle was Louis Carrogis; and that Louis Carrogis was the son of Philippe Carrogis, shoemaker, and of Marie-Jeanne Eybelly, his wife, a shoemaker's daughter, both resident in Paris at their shop in the rue du Cœur-Volant, at the corner of the rue des Quatre-Vents. Here, on the 15th of August 1717, Carmontelle was born, having for godfather a neighbouring grocer. To this modest origin and condition it is doubtless due that no particulars of the first forty years of his career are forthcoming, with exception of the fact that, in 1744, he stood sponsor for one of his brother's sons, being then described as Louis Carrogis, 'engineer'—a vocation presupposing, not only a specific technical training, but in addition some familiarity with geometry and mechanical drawing. He must at the same time have possessed, or afterwards acquired, the arts of etching and engraving, since there are said to be etchings signed L. Carrogis. Having for some time acted as tutor to the children of the Marquis d'Armentières, on the outbreak of the Seven Years' War he was carried by the commander of the Orléans regiment of dragoons, M. de Pons-Saint-Maurice, who was also Governor to the Duc de Chartres, into Westphalia, in the capacity of aide-de-camp. Here his chief duties were to draw military plans, carve cold turkey dexterously for his general officer, and make sketches—or, as they were then loosely styled, 'caricatures'—for the Duc de Chevreuse, of the respective officers of the Chevreuse, Bauffremont, Orléans, and Caraman troops of horse. These performances had already become numerous and popular, when, with the conclusion of the war, he was definitely attached to the household of the Duc d'Orléans, Louis-Philippe the First, familiarly known as the 'gros Duc,' under the title of Reader to his son, Louis-Philippe Joseph, Duc de Chartres, afterwards 'Égalité,' and then about sixteen. 'Quoique honorable,' says Mme. de Genlis, this was a post 'en quelque sorte subalterne,' and did not permit its holder even in the undress atmosphere of the Duke's country seats of St. Cloud or Villers-Cotterets, to take his meals with the family, although he seems later to have shared with the famous Tronchin, his Grace's physician-in-chief, the special privilege of eating ices in the evening with the rest of the court. But Carmontelle, for by this time he must long since have adopted his pseudonym, coupled with the much-suspected 'de' employed by Voltaire, was no ordinary man. He had, as we shall see, an imposing presence; his manners, without subserviency, were good; and, besides being exceptionally well-informed, he possessed many agreeable literary and social accomplishments, which must speedily have rendered him invaluable to a shifting and restless community of titled idlers, whose ceaseless inquiry, like that of Mme. de Genlis' M. Damézague, was 'Que férons-nous demain matin?' Foremost among these popular talents were the dramatic sketches, or 'Proverbes,' which later made him the Scribe of his epoch. It is, however, with his artistic gifts that we are here exclusively concerned. 'Il peignoit parfaitement [the epithet is of course exaggerated] à la gouache le paysage et la figure,' says his panegyrist; and he had the happy knack of taking full-length portraits, after the fashion introduced by Cochin, in profile, which made him much in requisition by the high-born or distinguished personages with whom he came in contact. Mme. de Genlis, whom he drew playing on the inevitable harp, says that he represented her as very ugly, and needlessly emphasized the height of her forehead. But there must assuredly have been some compensating qualities in the picture, for she shows no sign in her writing of the 'injuria spretæ formæ.' Another of Carmontelle's devices for amusing his contemporaries must have anticipated the modern moving-picture; and in some sort resembled those 'Ombres Chinoises' which Monsieur Séraphin was later to make so attractive a diversion of the reconstructed Palais Royal. Mme. de Genlis vaguely defines this as 'a sort of magic lantern.' Luckily, other reporters are more explicit. It consisted of a sequence of transparencies, or continuous designs on thin paper, the unrolling of which behind a glass revealed to the spectators on the other side an unending procession of figures of all sorts, occupied in all kinds of ways, and set in suitable landscapes or localities. Some of these transparencies are said to have been a hundred, or even a hundred and sixty feet long; and they afford an extraordinary testimony to the untiring industry and fertility of their contriver.[1] It is no wonder that such a man became in brief space 'Ordonnateur des fêtes en général' to the Duke of Orléans. For this office, coupled with his readership, he received the modest annual stipend of 1,800 livres, which, taking the livre to represent 10*d.* would mean £75. But he was apparently only on duty during 'la belle saison,' and it is but reasonable to assume that he was sometimes paid for his portraits.

For more than twenty years Carmontelle continued his unwearied and unambitious activities. Then, in 1785, the 'gros Duc' died, and was succeeded by Philippe 'Égalité.' By this date Carmontelle was nearing seventy. He seems, tempo-

[1] Angelo claims that his father did something of the same kind on the model of a pictorial drama entitled the 'Tableau mouvant,' which he had seen at Venice. 'He was so delighted with its effect, the scenes being painted as transparencies, and the figures being all black profiles, that he constructed a stage on the same plan, and it was greatly admired by Gainsborough, Wilson and other landscape painters.' ('Reminiscences,' 1830, i, 10.)

rarily at all events, to have passed to the service of the new Duke. But in 1785 the Revolution was in the near future; and henceforth we know little of his proceedings. He must, however, have contrived to preserve a 'juste milieu,' for, while most of his sitters emigrated or were guillotined, the storm rolled harmlessly over his head, leaving him impoverished but unscathed. He survived until December 1806, dying quietly at No. 22, Rue Vivienne, aged eighty-nine. In the register of the arrondissement, consulted by M. Jal, he is described as Louis Carrogis Carmontelle, 'célibataire' and 'rentier.' Of what his 'rentes' could have consisted, it is hard to conceive, if, as stated by some authorities, it be true that his closing years were spent in a state bordering on indigence; and that he was even obliged to pledge his MSS. at the Mont de Piété in order to meet a pressing necessity—one of those exceptional cases, adds the narrator sardonically, in which it has been found possible to raise money upon wit. It is further related that he often figured at the periodical free dinners which Mme. de Frénilly gave to her 'old and ruined friends'—dinners at which each guest 'ate to satisfy himself for the next few days.'[1] This was *c.* 1798. On the other

[1] 'Recollections of the Baron de Frénilly,' 1909, Heine-

hand, Mme. de Genlis, who saw Carmontelle frequently after 1802 at the apartments which Bonaparte had assigned to her in the Arsenal, declares that 'il jouissoit d'une honnête aisance.' 'Son caractère étoit si doux, ses mœurs si pures, ses talens si aimables, qu'il n'excita jamais la haine et l'envie. . . . Il fut toujours loué, aimé, considéré; et, dans un âge trés avancé, il termina paisiblement ses jours au sein de sa patrie.'

He had been in the habit of preserving the originals of his sketches, and of giving only copies to those of his sitters who wanted them. Consequently, at his death he possessed a large number of drawings, which were sold by auction in April 1807, a lengthy catalogue being printed at the Imprimerie des Sciences et des Arts. It described the collection as including 'seven hundred and fifty portraits of Princes and Lords, Princesses and titled Ladies, Ministers, Soldiers, Magistrates, Ecclesiastics, Savants, and illustrious Personages under the reign of Louis XV, painted in gouache from the life, and about eight or nine inches high.' M. Joly, the Keeper of the Prints at the Bibliothèque Impériale, was desirous that this unique gallery should be acquired by the

mann, p. 155. The hostess called these Saturday feasts 'jour d'ogres,' which her cook turned into 'jour de dogues.'

Government; but he unfortunately died before the purchase could be effected. Thereupon, 'a friend of Carmontelle, the Chevalier Richard de Lédans, a retired military man, well known to the Orléans family, determining that they ought not to be dispersed, borrowed the money to buy them, hoping he might be able to transfer them as a whole to one of Carmontelle's sitters, Talleyrand, by that time Bonaparte's Minister for Foreign Affairs. In this he was disappointed. He therefore sold a few of them separately,[1] thus reducing their number to five hundred and thirty sketches, comprising six hundred and thirty-five portraits. These he catalogued and classified, adding some prefatory account of Carmontelle, still preserved at the Musée Condé. As he himself had been familiar with many of the persons depicted, he was generally able to identify them. In 1816 Lédans died, and the collection passed into the hands of a certain Pierre de La Mésangère, a ci-devant priest and professor of belles-lettres at La Flèche, whom the Revolution had

[1] Possibly some of these reached the British Museum, which possesses four: the Duc de Chevreuse (hereafter mentioned), Mme. de Vermenoux, the Marquise de la Croix (a charming recumbent figure), and the 'Coureur' (messenger) of St.-Cloud.

transformed into the editor of the 'Journal des Dames et des Modes.' His knowledge of costume enabled him to add details to the labours of his predecessor, and to rectify minor mistakes; and he carefully mounted the drawings in their existing form. Then, in February 1831, La Mésangère also died, and on the 18th July his property, including the Carmontelle portraits, was dispersed by auction. At the Mésangère sale they were bought by the Gordon Duff family, and came to Banff. Here they remained until 1877, when their then-owner, Major Lachlan Gordon Duff of Drummuir, sold the majority of them[1] to Messrs. Colnaghi, from whom they eventually passed to Henri d'Orléans, Duc d'Aumale, King Louis-Philippe's fourth son, and the heir to the last of the Condés. The Duke had already contrived to secure some of Carmontelle's productions,[2] and he afterwards bought a few more.

[1] Major Gordon Duff retained a certain number, which are now in possession of his son, Mr. Thomas Gordon Duff. These include, among others, drawings of Hume, Talleyrand, the Duke of York, Bougainville the Elder, Mr. and Mrs. Wilkes, the Princesse de Salm and her son, the Duchesse de Chaulnes, and a very attractive 'laitière' of Villers-Cotterets.

[2] Some of these came from the sale of the concierge of the old Park or Garden of Monceau, which, in 1778, was

This brought the total up to four hundred and eighty-four drawings and five hundred and sixty-one portraits, which were re-arranged by a Brussels binder named Claessens in ten large red morocco volumes. These in 1897 the Duke bequeathed with the rest of his art treasures to the Institute of France. They are now in the Orléans salon of the Musée Condé, constituting a 'vast collection in which the second half of the eighteenth century lives again, with all its elegances and some also of its trivialities.'

The last words are quoted from the introduction

laid out for the Duc de Chartres by Carmontelle, who, though he declined to regard it as an English garden, decorated it freely with the temples, obelisks, Chinese bridges, and artificial ruins popular at Kew and Stowe. One of these structures, the Naumachia, an oval piece of water, partly encircled by a Corinthian colonnade, the fluted pillars of which came from the Valois tomb at St. Denis, still exists (Baedeker's 'Paris,' 1904, p. 217). The place was one of Carmontelle's favourite resorts, and he did numerous views for a volume describing it in 1779. In the delightful 'Nouvelles Promenades dans Paris' of M. Georges Cain, the curator of the Musée Carnavalet (p. 320), there is a plan showing that the original Parc Monceau, from which 'Égalité' and Lafayette heard the cannon announcing the fall of the Bastille, was as large again as the pretty well-kept pleasure-ground that now bears the name.

to a sumptuous quarto which, under the title of 'Chantilly: Les Portraits de Carmontelle,' Mons. F. A. Gruyer, the late accomplished curator of the Musée Condé, devoted to this particular branch of its riches; and to which we are indebted for many of the foregoing facts, since, although we have consulted numerous authorities (including of course our own favourite M. Jal), we have found it difficult to add much but those minor explanations always required in treating a French theme for English readers. Like the savant he was, M. Gruyer did his work 'savamment.' Besides all needful preliminaries, he gives ample information respecting the persons represented by Carmontelle, a task entailing no small labour: and what is more, he adds a number of photographic reproductions, which, to those who cannot make the pilgrimage to Chantilly, are of considerable value. That Carmontelle was an amateur must be admitted. But he certainly was not an amateur in the sense of the adage 'Qui dit amateur, dit ignorant.' On the contrary, he was abundantly instructed. His backgrounds and accessaries are always informing and appropriate; and his details of costume minutely studied. As to his likenesses, although he may not have satisfied the enthusiasm of Walpole or the vanity of Mme. de Genlis, there is no lack of testimony that he sufficiently met the requirements of ready recognition. As to this we may trust the ever-critical Grimm. 'He has the special gift of seizing the air, the carriage, the spirit of the figure rather than the resemblance of the features.[1] . . . Every day I find myself recognizing in society persons whom I have never seen except in his collections.' 'These, which he augments daily, also give an idea of the different states of life, as men and women of all degrees and ages enter into them indiscriminately, from Monsieur the Dauphin to the floor-polisher of St.-Cloud.' The quotation suggests a certain affinity with the work of the German Daniel Chodowiecki, and particularly with the sequence of drawings in the Berlin Academy which illustrate that artist's 'Journey to Danzig' in 1773, so excellently facsimiled by Messrs. Amsler and

[1] In confirmation of this M. Gruyer quotes from the Carmontelle sale catalogue of 1807 the description of a picture which represents six persons in the red St.-Cloud livery looking at a garden, with their backs to the spectator, each of whom it was easy to identify from his posture and general appearance. The very existence of such a drawing shows what was regarded as one of Carmontelle's special ingenuities. One remembers the wonderful hats in Hogarth's "Election Entertainment," all of which suggest different owners.

Ruthardt. Chodowiecki, with a wider inventive range, has all the sedulous fidelity to dress and accessary which distinguish his French contemporary. Indeed, at one point there is an actual though accidental connection between their labours. About 1765 Carmontelle made a design arising out of the well-known Calas case. Marc-Antoine Calas, a moody young fellow, had committed suicide; and the Roman Catholic fanatics of Toulouse persuaded themselves that, to prevent his turning Roman, he had been murdered by his Protestant father. The hapless old man was consequently broken on the wheel; but the rest of the family were exonerated; and Carmontelle's composition shows them receiving in prison the announcement of their acquittal. It is singularly effective, Mme. Calas and her two daughters being most sympathetically rendered, as well as their staunch fellow sufferer, the Roman Catholic servant. Of this drawing an excellent engraving by de La Fosse, published for the benefit of the sufferers, found its way to Berlin, and Chodowiecki copied it in oil. He then set about a pendant, depicting the condemned man's farewell to his family. This he himself engraved; and, as the print called the 'Adieux de Calas,' or 'Der grosse Calas' (to distinguish it from a smaller copy), it became one of the most famous of his productions.

M. Gruyer skilfully distributed the Carmontelle Gallery into groups of Princes and Princesses, Courtiers and Court Officials, Soldiers and Sailors, Great Ladies, Statesmen, Ecclesiastics, Authors, Musicians, and so forth. From so potent and reverend an assembly, one can but select for recognition, as one does in real life, a few of those whom one knows best or likes most. In such circumstances, we naturally look first for the person who, if not precisely the host, is certainly the 'ordonnateur de la fête': to wit—Carmontelle himself. He is not difficult to find, as he naturally figures in the group attached to the Orléans household. Seated on a terrace, with garden trees in the background, he is depicted in the act of taking one of the portraits to which, according to tradition, he was seldom able to devote more than a couple of hours. He is magnificently attired in a suit of garnet velvet, with green spots, and wears a bag of the same material. His hair is elaborately dressed in the fashion of 1762 or thereabouts, which would make him between forty and fifty. Before him, on an elegant Louis-Quinze table, lies the large book or album which Mme. de Genlis describes him as bringing into the room

CARMONTELLE: BY HIMSELF

(FROM GRUYER'S 'CHANTILLY: LES PORTRAITS DE CARMONTELLE' BY PERMISSION OF MM. PLON-NOURRIT ET CIE.)

at Villers-Cotterets after dinner in order to sketch the most recent arrivals. His artistic stock-in-trade is of the simplest. Red chalk for the flesh, black chalk for the dress; a little water or body colour for the final tints—this is all he wants. His appearance is that of a singularly methodical and self-possessed person, with comely features, and the air of a careful but calm investigator, of whom one may well believe, in Mme. de Genlis' words, that 'il joignait beaucoup de bonhomie à l'esprit le plus observateur, deux choses bien rarement réunies.'[1]

In royalties Carmontelle's gallery is not rich. Louis the Well-Beloved did not apparently figure among the sitters, nor need his absence be regretted. On the other hand, there is an excellent portrait of the unfortunate Dauphin, in queue and cadogan, with his hands buried in a muff. He is placed, like Carmontelle himself, on a terrace, with ominous cypresses in the background, although, in 1760, when this sketch was made, he had still five years before him; and was

[1] In 1762 he would be in his prime. Later reports describe him in advanced years somewhat differently. 'He was a thin man, with a long and severe face,' says Frénilly, 'a sardonic laugh, an imperious and choleric disposition; but hidden under this rugged exterior were a very good heart and a singularly lofty soul.' ('Recollections,' 1909, p. 5.)

apparently far from being the living ghost whom, not long before his death, Horace Walpole saw at Versailles. Carmontelle also drew the Dauphin's devoted German wife, mother of the sainted Mme. Elizabeth, and of three kings (Louis XVI, Charles X, and Louis XVIII); but her picture is not among the treasures of the Musée Condé. Other portraits in this group are Carmontelle's patron, the 'gros Duc,' that benevolent, albeit somewhat dull and prematurely portly personage, who afterwards married Mme. de Montesson, the aunt of whom Mme. de Genlis gives a so frankly feline account in her 'Memoirs' ('Elles se détestaient cordialement,' says Mme. d'Oberkirch); the Duc de Chartres, the 'gros Duc's' son, 'dans sa belle jeunesse,' which must have been the only thing beautiful that could ever be attributed to Philippe 'Égalité'; the Prince de Condé, not yet the leader of the émigrés of 1789, but the boy-hero of Johannisberg and the Seven Years' War, and 'Égalité's' sister, Thérèse-Bathilde d'Orléans, or 'Mademoiselle,' a very arch and winsome little lady, in all the bravery of panniers, powder, and begarlanded 'grand habit.'[1] But the most memor-

[1] 'Mademoiselle' married the Duc de Bourbon. Her only son was the ill-fated Duc d'Enghien, shot at Vincennes in 1804.

able pair in this category are 'Egalité's' sister-in-law, the hapless Princesse de Lamballe (of whom M. Gruyer does not reproduce the portrait), and her father-in-law, the good Duc de Penthièvre, about whose practical rather than pastoral benevolence his secretary Florian wrote:

> Bourbon n'invite pas les folâtres bergères
> À s'assembler sous les ormeaux;
> Il ne se mêle pas à leurs danses légères,
> Mais il leur donne des troupeaux.

It was the Duke's emissaries who tried to save the Princess at the terrible September massacres, but the butchers fell upon them with cries of 'Death to the disguised lacqueys of the Duc de Penthièvre,' and they themselves barely escaped.

From the dispersed and miscellaneous crowd of 'Personnages attached to the House of Orléans.' it is difficult to make selection. But it may be noted that several of them were English or Irish. Of Colonel Barré (perhaps the Isaac Barré who served under Wolfe against Rochfort), little is said beyond the fact that, besides being a gambler, he was a good amateur actor. General Clarke is another; but of the special functions of these two nothing is stated. There are also Lord Farnham, and the 'gros Duc's' preceptor, M. the Abbé

O'Mélan (?)—a 'très digne ecclésiastique,' and a 'très bon gentilhomme, comme tous les Irlandais du monde,' says Lédans, with a burst of enthusiasm. Then there are portraits of Count d'Adhémar, sometime ambassador to England; of another reader to the Duke d'Orléans, the vaudevillist, Collé, at this date a septuagenarian; of Mme. du Deffand's friend Pont-de-Veyle; of the Academician, La Curne de Sainte-Palaye, the author of the 'Dictionnaire des Antiquités Françaises.' But the most notable, and perhaps the most noteworthy historical figure is the famous Bailli de Suffren, one of the noblest names in French naval history, and the doughty opponent of Sir Edward Hughes in that long and changing struggle in East Indian waters which ended with the Peace of Versailles. The Bailli must have been among the last of Carmontelle's Orléans sitters, if his portrait be rightly dated 1785, since that was also the year of the 'gros Duc's' death. The number of portraits in this class is already too large to deal with; but it may be added that it is exceedingly comprehensive in its range, for it includes likenesses of the negroes, Narcisse and Auguste, of the latter of whom M. Gruyer says happily that 'il s'abandonne avec délices au plaisir de ne rien faire'; of Liennard Beller, the Suisse, whose duty, like that of Bousk at Versailles, was to fling open the folding doors and announce visitors in a stentorian voice; of the maître d'hôtel and the first valet de chambre; of the court tailor, and even the bird-boy ('garde-blés') of Villers-Cotterets.

To these worthies M. Gruyer devotes a number of pages, and there are more than three hundred in his bulky quarto volume. Of course, many of the personages described are obscure, and deservedly so. But with such a mass of material it is hopeless to cope in brief compass; and we must henceforth confine ourselves to the attractive section of 'Grandes Dames,' and to a few miscellaneous portraits, which, for one reason or another, present especial interest. In depicting the great ladies, Carmontelle, with his sense of grace, and his feeling for frippery must have taken unending delight. Many of his models were justly renowned for their beauty—the Duchesse de Chevreuse,[1] Mlle. de Bernay, Mme. du Tartre, the Comtesse

[1] The Duke's portrait is not at Chantilly, but, as already stated at p. 42 *n.*, in the British Museum. Husband and wife are each represented by simple drawings in black and red crayon; and both are dated 1758, during the Seven Years' War. The Duke's portrait was engraved by Auguste de Saint-Aubin.

d'Egmont, Marshal Richelieu's daughter and Walpole's friend, of whom, with her guitar, there is a graceful picture. Some, living life well even in a court, deserve our admiration for their purity: witness that admirable Comtesse de Séran—the Arethusa, or Margaret Godolphin, of a vicious Versailles, for all that she was witty as Mme. de Sévigné; others, the Duchesse de Lauzun, the Duchesse de Gramont, the Marquise du Plessis-Bellière, and Mme. de Saint-Amarant, compel consideration by the magnificent serenity with which they suffered on the scaffold. In a few of the drawings here reproduced, the composition includes several figures. One is an attractive group, consisting of the Presidente Lamoignon, a charming young mother of seven-and-twenty, with her four children, three girls and a boy—engaging little figures which not even lace caps and the proprieties of a Louis-Quinze costume can wholly deprive of their native artlessness; the other shows the Comtesse de Rumain, her eldest daughter the Comtesse de Polignac, and Mlle. de Rumain. This is a 'scène de salon.' The mother bends over the younger girl as she sits stiffly practising at what Tony Lumpkin calls the 'haspicolls'; the elder sister, a graceful figure, is working quietly on a tambour. Between the columns at the back you get a glimpse of a park. Turn the leaf, and you come on that emotional, clever Mlle. de Lespinasse, who behaved so ungratefully to Mme. du Deffand.[1] And very clever she looks in her dark dress and white lace, suggesting all the intellectual alertness for which she was renowned. 'She talked for the most part on plain subjects,' says the insensible Comte de Guibert for whom she sighed in secret, 'but she did not express herself in a common way, and this art, which seemed to be a second nature with her, never obtruded itself upon notice, and never led her into affectation.' Turn the leaf once more, and it is a stately Comtesse de Vauban, 'gathering rosebuds while she may,' in a 'robe, à double jupe et à volants,' with a stupendous 'head' and telescope curls ('rouleaux'), surmounted by a garland of eglantine, which again is crowned by a flutter of bone-lace lappets. But the details of costume would be interminable. Satins and taffeties, frills and furbelows, ribbons and flowers, ruches and 'plissés'—the bare enumeration would tax all the exact terminology of the Goncourts and the

[1] It is just possible that this portrait, a great favourite with Carmontelle, was done for Mme. du Deffand, as it is dated 1760, which comes within the ten years (1754-64) when the two ladies were still friends.

elegant science of M. Octave Uzanne. We must pass to our miscellaneous figures.

It has already been stated that Lédans, failing to find a purchaser for the Carmontelle gallery in Talleyrand, sold some of the drawings separately, which should account for the conspicuous absence of certain notable names. There is no portrait of Voltaire, for instance, in M. Gruyer's catalogue. But Carmontelle certainly drew Voltaire, since, as we shall see, the drawing has been engraved. Again, one might reasonably have looked for Rousseau, who was in Paris at the close of 1766. The only Rousseau mentioned, however, is Mme. Rousseau, wife of the famous 'maître d'armes des enfants de France,' to whom one of his judges, dismissing him to the guillotine, had the heartlessness to add 'Pare celle-ci, Rousseau!'—a barbarity worthy of Stevenson's Braxfield. Then there was certainly a Benjamin Franklin, for although it is not here reproduced, we have seen a copy of the engraving made from it, which is declared to be an excellent likeness, and represents him about 1780, when he was United States Minister.[1] But

[1] It is to be found among the portraits of Franklin included in the interesting facsimile of 'Poor Richard's Almanack for 1733,' issued by 'The Duodecimos' of New York, 1894, p. 48. The engraver was D. Née.

where there is so much, it is needless to note omissions. If there is no Voltaire, there is the Abbé de Voisenon, whom Voltaire perfidiously flattered; there are Grimm and Holbach, philosophes; there are Bachaumont and Duclos of the 'Memoirs'; there is M. de Buffon (in his literary velvet and laced ruffles, and wearing the Order of St. Michael); there is that patron of the arts, Mme. de Pompadour's brother, the Marquis de Marigny; there is the amiable Louis Racine, whose 'Memoir' of his now somewhat discredited father[1] was the favourite book of Rogers. Among the musicians is Rameau, a characteristic and long-legged figure, scribbling a score in front of his spinet; there is also a well-known Mozart group. The little boy of seven in an elaborate suit of sky-blue, trimmed with lace, and perched on a chair, the seat of which has been temporarily raised by cushions, is at the harpsichord; his sister, a girl of twelve, sings sedately by his side, while the father, Léopold Mozart, in red velvet, accompanies on the violin.[2]

[1] See 'Racine in the Dock,' by M. Augustin Filon, 'Fortnightly Review,' September 1911—a review of the recent study of the author of 'Athalie' by his great-grandson, M. Masson Forestier.

[2] 'Mozart, as a child,' also appears in B. Olivier's 'Thé à l'Anglaise chez le Prince de Conti' (that is—at the

But, to the English student, perhaps the most interesting portraits will be those of Garrick and Sterne. The two figures in the former represent the Garrick of Tragedy confronted by his second self, the Garrick of Comedy. Grimm's contemporary description puts this clearly: 'M. de Carmontelle,' he writes in July, 1765, 'has drawn Garrick in a tragic attitude, and facing this Garrick, he has placed, between two folding doors, a comic Garrick, who bursts upon the tragic Garrick and makes fun of him.'[1] Such a presentment of the great actor's dual personality is certainly a happy thought. The Sterne, which belongs to a somewhat earlier date (1762), is referred to in that writer's correspondence: 'The Duke of Orléans,' he tells Garrick, 'has suffered my portrait to be added to the number of some odd men in his collection; and a gentleman who lives with him has taken it most expressively.'

Palace of the Temple), now in the Musée du Louvre. He is playing the harpsichord, accompanied on the guitar by the singer Jélyotte. Several of Carmontelle's sitters are also present: the two Countesses d'Egmont, the Countess de Boufflers, the Duchess de Lauzun, the Prince de Conti, and M. Pont-de-Veyle.

[1] Grimm's 'Correspondance Littéraire.' Lédans says Carmontelle's drawing was made at the Orléans château of Le Raincy.

Expressive it assuredly is, and as fortunate as that of 'Roscius.' 'Yorick' is shown standing on the terrace of the Palais Royal (?), the dome of the Invalides (?) in the background. A tall, spare figure, with a sub-humorous look, he leans easily on a chair-back, one hand in his pocket, and he is decorously attired in a black suit, lace ruffles and a loose cravat. He has the long nose and the lips of the Nollekens terra-cotta of four years later, and it is probable that Carmontelle's is a closer likeness than the idealized Reynolds at Lansdowne House.[1]

What became of the popular transparencies, is doubtful. One of them is said to have been sold; but others, being included in the catalogue of 1807, must have been still undisposed of at Carmontelle's death. From a note by Mme. de Genlis, it would seem that negotiations were at one time on foot to sell them advantageously in Russia, though she had no further information on the subject.[2] The illustrations to the description

[1] Sterne speaks of obtaining an etching of the drawing, but this is unknown. The original portrait did not form part of the Lédans collection. It was bought separately in London by the Duc d'Aumale for £64. A few copies were issued in 1890 by Messrs. Colnaghi.

[2] See Appendix A (Carmontelle's Transparencies).

of the Park of Monceau have already been referred to.[1] But a closing word must be devoted to the other engravings after Carmontelle's drawings, some of the originals of which are in the Musée Condé, and some not. The bulk of these were by Jean-Baptiste-Joseph de La Fosse, the engraver of 'La Malheureuse Famille Calas.' He is credited among other things with a portrait of the 'gros Duc' on horseback, in hunting costume, and duly furnished with the regulation cor-de-chasse; with portraits of the Duke and the Duc de Chartres in a billiard-room; of Rameau; of the Abbé de Chauvelin, and of the Mozart group. Other engravers who copied Carmontelle were Houel, Miger, Auguste de Saint-Aubin, J. B. Tilliard ('Pas de Deux'), and Nicolas Ransonnette. To Carmontelle himself are assigned etchings of the Abbé Allaire, 'Egalité's' preceptor; of the Baron de Besenval, familiar in Carlyle; and of Voltaire, walking in the neighbourhood of 'Les Délices.' Carmontelle also executed a plate of 'La Bouquetière' after Boucher. But his fame as an artist will rest mainly on the series of portraits in the Musée Condé, a standing testimony

[1] Two of these, the Naumachia and the Temple of White Marble, are reproduced in Cain's 'Nouvelles Promenades dans Paris,' *n.d.*, pp. 322, 326.

to his exceptional gift of accurate observation, his extraordinary fertility, and his no less extraordinary industry. If his work never attained the level of excellence which gives it the stamp of genius, it was of no small service to his contemporaries; and it is still of enduring interest to the historian, the antiquary, and the archæologist.[1]

[1] Since this paper first appeared in the 'National Review' for June, 1911, a long and interesting article on Carmontelle, under the title of 'Un Amuseur Oublié,' has been contributed to the 'Revue des Deux Mondes,' by M. Augustin Thierry (15th April, 1912).

GARRICK'S 'GRAND TOUR'

WITH Davies and Murphy, with Boaden's bulky 'Correspondence,' with the two lives of Mr. Percy Fitzgerald, and the compact monograph of the late Joseph Knight, it might not unreasonably be supposed that Garrick material, in spite of its extent, had already been sufficiently exploited. But whether the much-suspected final word has, or has not, been uttered, it must be granted that discussion of a subject from a fresh standpoint is never wholly out of date. While there are German inquirers and French appraisers (and indications are not wanting that each is learning something from the methods of the other), we may always be glad to welcome a supplementary study of Garrick, either Teutonic or Gallic, feeling assured that English writers, as well as readers, could not fail of instruction. Great biographers we have, living and dead; but it can scarcely be asserted that in this particular department the general level of craftsmanship is unimpeachable; or that performances such as the Burns of the late M. Auguste Angellier, or the

Crabbe of M. Réné Huchon, are turned out by the dozen in our favoured land. Then, in addition to the new survey or the neglected aspect, there is the separate treatment of episodes or incidents with which a foreigner, should his own country or customs be concerned, is naturally better qualified to deal than an outsider. Rousseau or Voltaire in England are themes more suited to an Englishman than to a Frenchman: Sterne or Garrick in France, on the contrary, may offer greater facilities to a Frenchman than an Englishman. In the case of Sterne, something has been done by the capable volume issued by M. Paul Stapfer in 1870; but, in our own day, it has been reserved for Mons. F. A. Hedgcock, 'Docteur-ès-Lettres' of the Sorbonne, to turn his special attention to Garrick's experiences abroad.[1]

To Garrick, then, as seen for the moment through alien glasses, this latest inquiry is confined. Its author does not contemplate another

[1] 'David Garrick et ses Amis Français,' by F. A. Hedgcock, 1911. This was a thesis presented to the University of Paris for the 'Doctorat-ès-Lettres. M. Hedgcock, who is English by birth, and 'doctus sermones utriusque linguae,' has recently translated it, with additions (Stanley Paul and Co.). He is now lecturer in French literature in the University of Birmingham.

life of the great 'acteur cosmopolite,' as he styles him; but he professes, from sources published and unpublished, to trace out the story of Garrick's relations with the French comedians who in 1749 visited London, and also of his travels on the Continent in 1763-5. With this object M. Hedgcock has diligently examined the numerous letters written by foreigners in the thirty-five volumes of Garrick's Correspondence at South Kensington—a mine until now more prospected than explored. And to the result of his investigations, he has prefixed such a brief biographical introduction and general estimate as serve to explain and illustrate Garrick's position with respect to his Gallic contemporaries. But even this modest design affords him an opportunity of rectifying some of the undetected lapses of his forerunners. Of these corrections, the most notable is contained in an appendix to his opening chapter, disposing of the claim—never it seems put forward seriously by the actor himself—to noble French extraction. His alleged connection with the Perigourdin De la Garrigues turns out to be as unsupported as Fielding's supposed descent from the Habsburgs, since reference to the marriage register of his grandfather, David Garric, proves conclusively that the said grandfather was a Protestant 'bourgeois et marchand' of Bordeaux la Bastide; and that his wife, Jeanne, was the daughter of Jean Sarrazin, also a 'marchand,' of Pons in Saintonge. In other words, the immediate ancestors of our English Roscius were frankly middle-class and commercial; and of 'sangre azul,' as the Spaniards call it, there is no distinguishable trace. But Huguenot and Bordelais, with a dash of Irish vivacity from the maternal side, is by no means a bad histrionic blend.

Future English writers on Garrick will do wisely to note this little amendment of an oft-repeated statement, unless indeed they are in a position to contradict it—a rather remote contingency. But it is beside M. Hedgcock's intention to pick holes in Garrick's pedigree; and this is only a casual detail of the chapter prefacing his main purpose. In the same chapter he also touches briefly on Garrick's aspects as actor, Shakespeare-lover and author. As author he counts least. A fortunate epigram or a happily turned prologue does not make a poet. Nor can it be pretended that adaptations from the French, however adroit, constitute stagecraft; and it is to be noted that, in 'The Clandestine Marriage,' the only one of Garrick's pieces which has passed into the répertoire, the elder Colman was his collaborator.[1] Of his abridgments and readjustments of Shakespeare's text, apart from his impersonation of Shakespeare's characters, the less said the better, although, having regard to the French influence they betray, they cannot be entirely disregarded. But as an actor, there is no doubt as to his undisputed supremacy; and M. Hedgcock's quotations from Grimm and Préville show how thoroughly this was recognized by his admirers of Outre-Manche. What seems to have struck them most was the mar-

[1] It is true that he is credited with more quoted passages than some greater men. But his jewels are mostly old gems re-set. His 'fellow-feeling makes one wondrous kind,' comes virtually, like Captain Shandon's Greek and Latin, from Burton's 'Anatomy'; and, as pointed out in a later paper in this volume, his oft-cited couplet on the fugitive nature of the actor's art had been anticipated by Robert Lloyd. One of his less known couplets opens the 'Prologue' to that hapless 'Virginia' of Fanny Burney's 'Daddy Crisp':

PROLOGUES, like compliments, are loss of time;
'Tis penning bows, and making legs in rhyme.

The manuscript of the 'Clandestine Marriage,' it may be added, partly in Colman's and partly in Garrick's handwriting, was recently on sale in London. It has now gone —where so many good things now go—to America.

vellous versatility which enabled him to pass instantaneously from comedy to tragedy, or vice versa.[1] And the additional fact that, like Rousseau, very few of his audience could have understood English, is a standing proof of that extraordinary facial power to which so many have testified from Johnson to Lichtenberg. Grimm's words are not new; but they will bear repetition; and we make a somewhat longer quotation than M. Hedgcock: 'It is easy to contort one's face; that may be conceived; but Garrick knows neither grimace nor exaggeration; all the changes that take place in his features arise out of the manner in which he is affected internally: he never exceeds the truth; and he knows that other inconceivable secret of improving his appearance without other aid than passion. We have seen him play the dagger scene in the tragedy of 'Macbeth,' in a room, in his ordinary dress, without any help from theatrical illusion; and in proportion as with his eyes he followed

[1] Sterne confirms this in a letter to Garrick from Paris of 10th April 1762: ''Tis the greatest problem in nature, in this meridian, that one and the same man should possess such tragic and comic powers, and in such an equilibrio, as to divide the world for which of the two Nature intended him. ('Works,' 1798, ix, 78.)

this dagger hanging and moving in the air, his expression became so fine ['il devenait si beau'] as to extract a general cry of admiration from all the assembly. Will it be credited that this same man, a moment afterwards, imitates with equal perfection a pastry-cook's boy, who, gaping about him in the street, his stock-in-trade on his head, lets his tray tumble in the gutter, and dumbfounded at first with his accident, ends by bursting into tears.[1]

Another testimony, that of the famous Préville —'Mercury himself,' Sterne calls him—is less known. After speaking of the actor's obligation to assume all parts, he says: 'Nature is niggard of these phenomena, who appear once in a century, and such, incontestably, is a comedian so endowed. For our century this phenomenon was reserved to England: Garrick had no rival in any country, and the title [of Roscius] which

[1] Grimm, 'Corr. Litt.,' July, 1765. The pieman's misadventures must have been a never failing contemporary jest. In Hogarth's 'Four Times of the Day,' 1738, a boy is shown crying uproariously because he has broken the dish he is bringing from the baker's by setting it down too smartly on a post; and in the 'March to Finchley,' 1750, a pieman, with a tray on his head, is being robbed by a man who is insidiously drawing his attention to a trick played on a milkmaid.

THE TWO GARRICKS: BY CARMONTELLE

FROM GRUYER'S 'CHANTILLY: LES PORTRAITS DE CARMONTELLE'
BY PERMISSION OF MM. PLON-NOURRIT ET CIE.)

he merited is still unclaimed.'[1] Probably it was this peculiar mobility of feature which led Carmontelle, in his Chantilly portrait, to depict Garrick, in one and the same design, as comedian and tragedian. Indeed (although the point does not appear to have been noted), the posture and gestures of the tragic Garrick are precisely those which he might have been expected to assume in the aforementioned scene from 'Macbeth.' He is certainly looking at something in the air, and not at his comic double.[2]

With Garrick's personality we may now however dispense, and pass to his foreign friends. Foremost of these was one Jean Monnet, whose very chequered experiences as page to the Duchess of Berry, printer, author, Trappist, prisoner in

[1] 'Memoirs' of Préville, 1823.

[2] See *ante*, p. 58. There is a passage in Diderot's 'Paradoxe sur le Comédien' which is worth quoting in this connection: 'Garrick will put his head between two folding doors, and in the course of five or six seconds his expression will change successively from wild delight to temperate pleasure, from this to tranquillity, from tranquillity to surprise, from surprise to blank astonishment, from that to sorrow, from sorrow to the air of one overwhelmed, from that to fright, from fright to horror, from horror to despair, and thence he will go up again to the point from which he started. (W. H. Pollock's translation, 1883, p. 38.)

the Bastille, Director of the Théâtre de la Foire (de Saint Germain), and so forth, had brought him at last in 1749 to London with a troupe of French actors. He had come at the invitation of John Rich, the manager of Covent Garden; but Rich, alarmed by some ominous indications of Gallophobia, withdrew from his bargain. Thereupon Monnet, at a nonplus, turned to Garrick, who befriended him, with the result that Monnet and his company opened the little theatre in the Haymarket. Rich's apprehensions were by no means groundless. The first representation closed ignobly with a dispute between the boxes and the gallery; and silence was only secured for the second by a formidable cohort of hired butchers and watermen. Finally the Lord Chamberlain stopped the performance; and Monnet had to console himself as he could with the subventions of his supporters, and a benefit generously bestowed on him by Garrick. The result of these things was a lifelong friendship between the two men; and there are some fifty of Monnet's letters to Garrick in the Forster Collection. Henceforth it is Monnet who becomes, so to speak, Garrick's indefatigable agent and Paris correspondent. 'Coiffures' and laces for Mrs. Garrick; new plays and engravings for her husband; dancers, cooks, jewellers, professors of French—in all these matters Monnet is the adviser and universal provider; and the more devoted and assiduous, because, before a few years are over, his regained position as Director of the Opéra Comique has left him an enriched and unoccupied man.[1] He gave Garrick invaluable aid in the lighting and decorating of Drury Lane; and it was to Monnet that Garrick was indebted for an introduction to one of his most useful coadjutors, Casanova's pupil, the painter Philip de Loutherbourg, who eventually became superintendent of the scenery and machinery of the theatre. More than one of Garrick's occasional pieces owed their existence, if not their origin, to the effective picture-setting of de Loutherbourg. A second notability whom Monnet sent to Garrick was the pyrotechnist, Torré, to whose Marylebone Garden fireworks Dr. Johnson unkindly, and quite indefensibly, compared the metrical 'coruscations' of the author of 'An Elegy in a Country Church Yard.' Lastly, it was through Monnet that Garrick made the acquaintance of yet another luminary of Marylebone, Haydn's friend, Barthélémon the violinist,

[1] One of C. N. Cochin's profiles, excellently engraved by Saint-Aubin, gives an attractive idea of Monnet. It has also a neatly appropriate motto: '*Mulcet, movet, monet.*'

who, beginning as leader of the band there, ended by conducting the orchestra at Vauxhall.

To visit Monnet, Garrick, in all probability, made his first journey to Paris, taking with him his wife, Eva Maria Violette, to whom he had been married two years before; and 'who (adds Davies) from the day of her marriage to the death of her husband, had never been separated from him for twenty-four hours.' One of his fellow travellers is said to have been Sir George Lewis, afterwards murdered in the Forest of Bondy.[1] Another 'compagnon de voyage' was 'M. Denis,' who *may* have been that Charles Denis, the later friend of Churchill and Robert Lloyd, whom the latter fondly regarded as 'La Fontaine by transmigration'—a description which, judging from the versions in the 'St. James's Magazine,' sug-

[1] With this event is associated one of the numerous legends arising out of Garrick's remarkable mimetic powers. The suspected murderer, an Italian count, was on the point of being released for want of evidence, when Garrick, making up as the dead man, extorted from the terrified criminal an admission of his guilt. The story is on a par with that later fable of the journalist de la Place, which represents Garrick as impersonating Fielding long after his death, in order to prove that, in this way, he had helped Hogarth to recall the features—the very marked features, be it added—of his former friend.

gests an imperfect estimate of the supreme art of the French 'conteur.' It is unfortunate that Garrick's journal of 1751 has been lost, as this fact, coupled with the fact that the record was probably restricted to Monnet's circle, has of necessity limited M. Hedgcock's investigations. As regards Garrick's presentation to Louis XV, M. Hedgcock has discovered no confirmatory evidence. But he has disinterred from the 'Journal' of the vaudevillist, Charles Collé—who is his authority for the mention of Denis, and who, like Carmontelle, was one of the readers to the 'gros Duc' of Orléans—an entry relating to a meeting on 12th July, between the 'French Anacreon' and the 'English Roscius.' Garrick acted for Collé the famous dagger-scene, of which Grimm's account has already been quoted; and Collé's recollections fully bear out Grimm's report. 'He [Garrick] filled us with terror; it is not possible to depict a situation better, to render it with greater warmth, and at the same time to be more self-possessed.'[1] 'He considers all our actors more

[1] At this date, it should be observed that, although some of Shakespeare's plays had been poorly translated by de la Place, Shakespeare was little known in France generally. The inadequate 'Hamlet' of Ducis (who had no English) was not acted until 1769; his 'Roméo et Juliette' in 1772; his 'Lear' in 1783, and his 'Macbeth' in 1784.

or less bad (Collé continues); and in this respect we say ditto to him.' But Garrick must have made exception in favour of Mlle. Clairon, whose merits afterwards conquered both Goldsmith and Gibbon.[1] With some professional reservations, he greatly admired her; and predicted for her the more distinguished future she achieved.

His correspondence contains but one reference to this expedition; and that is in a letter to his brother Peter, apparently written, after his return to England, from Lord Burlington's house at Chiswick: 'You ask me (he says) how I like France? It is ye best place in the World to make a Visit to & I was indeed much satisfy'd with my Journey. . . . I had much honour done me both by French & English; & Every body and Thing contributed to make me happy. The great fault of our Countrymen is, y^t^ when they go to Paris, they keep too much among themselves, but if they would mix wth ye French as I did, it is a most agreeable Jaunt.' When Garrick left Paris, and whether his departure was in any way connected with a frustrated project for attracting French talent to London, an enterprise in which the 'prévôt des marchands' found it

[1] Goldsmith's 'Bee,' 1759, No. 2; Gibbon's 'Autobiographies,' 1896, pp. 204, 262.

necessary to intervene, it is impossible to say. In any case, he was back in England in July 1751.

A period of more than twelve years elapsed before he again crossed the Channel. But in the interval he added two to the list of his French friends, of whom one, by the promise of his brief life, deserves a passing mention. This was Claude-Pierre Patu, a consumptive young advocate and dramatist, much interested in England, and an enthusiast in Shakespeare and Garrick. At the end of 1754, in spite of the fogs, he came to London for a few weeks, assiduously frequenting Drury Lane Theatre. He speedily grew intimate with the accessible actor, who received him with 'une politesse vraiment française'; and, going back to France, began, like Monnet, to correspond regularly with his new friend on matters theatrical and literary. He showed much attention to Garrick's colleague, Mrs. Pritchard, when she visited Paris with her daughter; he assisted in negotiating between Garrick and the dancer Noverre. One of his projects, anticipating Johnson, was to write, in conjunction with Garrick, a 'Parnasse Anglois,' or Lives of the British Poets, which was to reveal to his benighted countrymen the unsuspected riches of our insular muse. To Fréron's 'Journal Étranger' he contributed papers on many English subjects—Mrs. Charlotte Lenox's 'Shakespeare Illustrated,' the 'Barbarossa' of Dr. Brown of the 'Estimate' (that 'Barbarossa' whose midnight bell was so dear to Johnson's 'Dick Minim'!), the alterations of Garrick in 'Romeo and Juliet,' and (perhaps) a version of Garrick's adaptation of Motteux, the 'Lying Valet.' But in 1756, he certainly issued anonymously, under the title 'Choix de Petites Piéces du Théâtre Anglais,'[1] two volumes of translations of English Plays, the second of which consisted of the 'Beggar's Opera' and the 'What d'ye Call It' of Gay, whom he greatly admired. Patu must have been a singularly engaging personage, since he succeeded in conciliating both Voltaire and Fréron; and he even contrived, at the Délices, to

[1] This was not the first translation, for, strangely enough, it was with a version made (says Patu) 'by a German who knew neither English nor French,' that in 1749 Monnet's company had attempted to attract an English audience. Patu's rendering (now before us) is a creditable production, usefully annotated. He also translated, in his first volume, Dodsley's 'Toy-Shop,' 'King and the Miller of Mansfield,' and 'Blind Beggar of Bethnal Green,' as well as Coffey's popular 'Wives Metamorphosed,' some of which pieces found imitators in France. Sedaine's 'Diable à Quatre,' for instance, is based on Coffey.

champion that 'amiable barbarian,' Shakespeare. Until M. Hedgcock and M. Huchon discovered him, little seems to have been known of him; and though Boaden prints his letters, French and English, Garrick's English biographers never mention his name. Unhappily, he was of those whom the Fates but show to mankind, for he died prematurely of decline in 1757. To England he never returned; but he retained his predilection for us to the end; and his final missive to Garrick from Naples in November 1756, the last of a packet which the actor had labelled 'Poor Patu's Letters,' closes with the Ghost's farewell in 'Hamlet'—'Adieu! *Remember me*!'

Jean-Georges Noverre, or the 'Chevalier' Noverre, another of Garrick's French friends at this date, is not at the altitude of Patu, although as a popular 'maître-de-ballet,' he was naturally more widely known. He had been introduced to Garrick by Monnet, one of whose company he had been at the Thèâtre de la Foire. In 1754 he had delighted the Parisians by two elaborate choregraphic entertainments, both described as triumphs of artful variety and ingenious combination—the 'Fêtes Chinoises' and the 'Fontaine de Jouvence.' Garrick endeavoured to secure the 'Chinese Festival' troupe for Drury

Lane; and after protracted preliminaries with Noverre, who, being a Swiss, developed all the mercenary aptitudes of his race, they arrived in London in November 1755. But the moment was singularly ill chosen. England was on the eve of that Seven Years' War whose origin so perplexed the eminent historian, Mr. Barry Lyndon; and animosity to 'insulting Gaul' was —especially among the lower classes—in its acutest stage. It was idle to protest to an unreasoning mob that Noverre was of another nationality; as Foote said later in the 'Minor,' the 'patriot gingerbread baker from the Borough' would not suffer 'dancers from Switzerland, because he hated the French.' Even though George II attended the first representations of the 'Chinese Festival,' there were disturbances at the outset, which increased in intensity with every renewal of the performance. Constant collisions took place between the rival factions; blows were exchanged, swords drawn, benches torn up, mirrors and lustres smashed, and not a few persons maimed or injured. On the 18th, the disorder reached its culminating point. The unfortunate dancers were assailed with a storm of peas and tin-tacks; and as soon as the pit was cleared by the boxes, it was re-captured by the gallery. At last a battalion of hired bruisers, entering the theatre, ejected the malcontents, who hurried off vindictively to smash Garrick's windows, and, if possible, burn his house in Southampton Street. So ended a fortnight's scandal. Garrick seems nevertheless to have behaved liberally to Noverre, although he had suffered heavily by the damage to his property; and it is to Noverre's subsequent 'Lettres sur les Arts imitateurs' that we owe one of the best and most detailed accounts of Garrick's acting. It is too lengthy to reproduce entire; but it is the report of an expert eye-witness; and one or two passages confirming what has already been said may find a place here: 'He [Garrick] was so natural, his expression had so much truth, his gestures, his physiognomy, and his looks were so eloquent and so persuasive, that they placed even those who knew no English in possession of the facts of the story. He could be followed easily; he touched in the pathetic; in the tragic he aroused all the successive emotions of the most violent passions. . . . In the higher comedy he captivated and entranced; in the lesser kind he amused; and he transformed himself in the theatre with so much art that he was often unrecognized by persons who habitually lived with him. . . . He may, without partiality, be regarded as the Roscius of England, because with diction, delivery, fire, nature, wit and delicacy, he combined that pantomime and that rare expression of dumb show which characterize the great actor and the complete comedian.'

Noverre, it is safe to infer, owed much to Garrick; and it was from Garrick that he learned the sovereign use of gesture and expression, even in dancing.

With May 1756 the Seven Years' War began, and further trips to France had to be indefinitely postponed, though Garrick often cast a longing eye across the Channel, and even during the progress of hostilities cherished vague projects for re-visiting his French friends. At the Peace of Paris all these inclinations revived with new pertinacity, heightened by the reports of Sterne, who preceded him by several months. He was grievously in want of change; his sleepless energy had impaired his health; he was fretted by petty cabals and jealousies, and, excellent actor though he was, the fickle public had grown a little weary of him. Consequently, leaving Drury Lane to his partner Lacy and his brother George, with Colman for literary assessor, he started for the Continent in September 1763, carrying with him

Mrs. Garrick and his pet dog, Biddy. Four days later he reached the French capital. His first visit was to the Théâtre français, of which he was straightway made free. Here Mlle. Dumesnil was acting in La Chaussée's 'crying comedy' of 'La Gouvernante'; and apparently struck Garrick chiefly by what Gibbon calls her 'intemperate sallies.' 'She made use,' Garrick wrote, 'of little startings and twitchings, which are visibly artificial, and the mere mimicry of the free, simple, and noble working of the passions.'[1] He called on Préville; and on Mlle. Clairon, of whose marked advance in her new manner he had heard from Sterne. 'She is highly improved since you saw her,' Yorick had said. But the 'Blanche et Guiscard' of Saurin, then being played at the Comédie, a version of Thomson's 'Tancred and Sigismunda' in which Garrick himself had often acted Tancred, was not one of her successes, although, if we are to believe Bachaumont's 'Mémoires Secrets,' he gave her hints. This may have been the case, as the rehearsals were in progress when he arrived. But he is discreetly silent as to the piece and her part in it.

Shortly after its production at the close of

[1] Fitzgerald's 'Garrick,' 1899, p. 284.

September, he must have left Paris for Italy, going first to Lyons; and it was more than a year before he saw Paris again. Making his way from Lyons to Turin, he sent a gossiping letter to his brother George, asking for news of the theatre; begging him to forward Churchill's 'Ghost' (presumably Book IV, the last published); warning him not to let the sun spoil Hogarth's Election pictures (then hanging in the bow-room at Hampton House), and so forth. Perhaps the most important item of intelligence in this communication is the announcement that Voltaire has warmly invited him to visit Ferney, a pleasure which he proposes to defer until his return from Italy. But he is clearly much disturbed by Voltaire's declaration, in the 'Essai sur les Moeurs et l'Esprit des Nations,'[1] that there was 'more *Barbarism* than *Genius* in Shakespeare's works.' From Turin the Garricks passed to Milan; next to Genoa and Florence, where they were welcomed by Frederick the Great's Chamberlain, the poet Francesco Algarotti, then ill and failing. Garrick recommended him to try that rival in popularity to Dr. James's Fever Powder, the Tar Water of Bishop Berkeley. But tar water helped the poor 'Swan of Padua'

[1] Works, 1819, vol. xv, p. 94.

as little as it had helped Fielding, for Algarotti died in the following year, on the very day that he had written for Garrick an introduction to some of his friends at his old home, Bologna. After a fortnight's sight-seeing in Rome the travellers went on to the Christmas festivities at Naples, whence arrive to George Garrick fresh accounts of the grand people who were everywhere fêting and flattering his illustrious brother —Lord and Lady Spencer, Lord Exeter, Lady Orford (Horace Walpole's erratic sister-in-law), Lord Palmerston—and of endless balls, suppers and masquerades. He has 'forgot England, and all his trumpery at Drury Lane.' He is collecting musical data for Burney; he has made the acquaintance of the two Dances, one of whom Nathaniel (afterwards Sir Nathaniel Dance Holland), was to paint him most successfully—far more successfully than Hogarth—as Richard III. He has seen all the curiosities of the neighbourhood; and in the Elysian Fields at Baiae has been so 'very near wet to the skin,' that he was incapacitated for enjoying either Caesar's Palace or Tully's villa.[1]

[1] Garrick's little foibles are so familiar that it is only fair to clear him of things 'not proven.' He had been annoyed, this letter shows, by some gossip in the 'St.

April finds him once more at Rome, where Dance paints, and Nollekens (then six-and-twenty) models a first bust of him. In May he is at Parma, doing the dagger scene for the Duke of York and an illustrious party—'mouthing for snuff-boxes,' as one of his company afterwards irreverently put it, in reference to a present he received on this occasion. Then he follows the Duke to Venice, from which place he writes again in June to George Garrick. Both he and his wife are unwell; and they are to try the mud baths of Abano. The régime seems to have suited the lady; but her husband was not equally fortunate. 'I eat and drink too much and laugh from morning to night,' he had written from Naples. The reviser of 'Romeo and Juliet' should have remembered that 'violent delights have violent ends.' By the time (August 1764) he had reached his next stage, Munich, he was

James's Chronicle' about his 'dancing with ye Duke of Devonshire.' Hitherto it has been too hastily assumed that 'Duke' was a mistake for 'Duchess,' with the corollary that Garrick himself sent the story to press. But M. Hedgcock, conscientiously consulting the statement in situ, discovers it to be an entirely fictitious account of an imaginary fête in honour of the Peace, at which, among other things, Mr. Garrick and his Grace were to figure in a country-dance!

seriously ill. 'The excellent Continental cookery, the long sequence of banquets in which he had taken part, Florence wine, and the hours spent in a gondola under the oppressive Venetian atmosphere [these are M. Hedgcock's inexorable words!] had ended by producing their effect.' That is to say—he was laid up for five weeks with severe bilious fever. He was so bad that he sketched his own epitaph, which would have been more affecting, were it not probable that the whole twelve lines were composed for the sake of the last two:

> Much-honoured Camden was my friend,
> And Kenrick was my foe.

His illness pulled him down considerably, and he was apparently growing homesick. September found him at Augsburg debating whether he should join the Duke of Devonshire at 'The Spaw,' or pay his promised visit to Voltaire. The sudden death of the Duke on 3rd October settled one proposition; and, owing to the state of his health, he determined to abandon the other. In a highly alembicate epistle, the much-corrected drafts of which are at South Kensington, he excused himself to the autocrat of Ferney, who, among other things, had politely offered his expected guest the use of his little private theatre. He should have been happy indeed (Garrick wrote) could he have been the means of bringing Shakespeare into some favour with M. de Voltaire. 'No enthusiastick Missionary who had converted the Emperor of China to his religion would have been prouder than I, could I have reconcil'd the first Genius of Europe to our Dramatick faith.' To this, after his fashion, he added a qualifying postscript: 'Tho I have called Shakespeare our dramatick faith yet I must do my country-men the Justice to declare that notwithstanding their deserv'd admiration of his astonishing Powers they are not bigotted to his errors, as some French Journalists have so confidently affirm'd.'

In the course of October he arrived at Paris, the air of which, says Grimm, perfectly restored him: and for the next six months, despite the strain of his illness, he continued a flattered centre of attraction. He took a convenient first floor in the Rue St. Nicaise close to the Tuileries; and the salons of philosophedom at once flung open their doors to him. At the rue Sainte Anne, Helvétius and his wife welcomed him in their magnificent hotel, then the rendezvous of all the notabilities. 'There,' says M. Hedgcock, in a carefully wrought passage, 'he meets Diderot, the irrepressible, the inquiring, ready to discuss everything, flitting from one subject to another with astounding rapidity; D'Alembert, the decoy-bird of the dinner-table, the wittiest of talkers, who, after a morning spent over mathematical problems, came to chat of acting with the English visitor; the handsome Marmontel, moderately gifted but much satisfied with himself; Saint-Lambert, cold, affected, very picked of speech; Grimm, the keen critic, collecting on all sides the material for his "Correspondance Secrète"; the Abbé Morellet, whom Voltaire, for his causticity, nicknamed "the Abbé Mord-les," and others beside who composed [what Garat calls] the "États généraux de l'esprit humain."'[1]

Another of the houses where he was cordially received was that of the author of the 'Système de la Nature,' Baron d'Holbach, where, in addition to most of the foregoing, he met the impressionable ex-actress and author, Mme. Riccoboni, afterwards a firm friend and one of the most constant, if most impulsive, of his correspondents. A third rallying-place was the historic salon, in the rue St. Honoré, of that 'mère nourrice

[1] In his English edition M. Hedgcock has expanded this; but we preserve our version of the original passage.

des philosophes,' Mme. Geoffrin, whose wit and conversation attracted not only Hume and Walpole, but Wilkes and Adam Smith. Here Garrick found sculptors and artists; and it was doubtless to this time that he owed his acquaintance with Joseph Vernet, the friend of Mme. Vigée-Lebrun; with Hubert Bourguignon, otherwise Gravelot, and with the statuary, J. B. Le Moyne, who exhibited a bust of him at the Salon of 1765.

In this congenial company Garrick was thoroughly at home. He was of French extraction; he spoke French as fluently as his wife spoke German; his vivacity, his tact, his insatiable 'désir de plaire,' were all recommendations to admirers already prepossessed in his favour. He wanted no pressing to exhibit his talents—made no pretence of hesitation; but was ready at a moment's notice to gratify a sympathetic audience. 'Without waiting for the wish to become a petition, alone and surrounded by faces that almost touched his own, he played the greatest scenes of the English stage. His ordinary coat or cloak, his hat and his boots or shoes, as he arranged them, became the best conceivable costumes for every possible rôle.'[1] For the benefit of listeners his

[1] Garat, 'Mémoires historiques sur le XVIII Siècle, etc.,' 1821, Bk. v.

words were sometimes rapidly paraphrased in French by the journalist Suard; but it was needless. 'The pantomime of Garrick was the noblest, the most energetic, the most pathetic of translations.' In regard to this, M. Hedgcock relates once more the oft and variously told story of the friendly contest between Garrick and Mlle. Clairon at the house of Mr. Neville of the Embassy. Mlle. Clairon, to draw Garrick out, recited passages from Racine and Voltaire: Garrick responded with the dagger scene and the soliloquy in 'Hamlet.' Then, going on to the madness of Lear, he incidentally informed the company what had first taught him to depict it. It was the recollection of the poignant distress of an unhappy father who, by accident, had dropped his child from a window. And presently, leaning over the back of a chair, he re-enacted the whole scene—the father's agony, horror, insanity—with such tremendous effect that, as Murphy says, 'tears gushed from every eye in the room.' 'Never have I seen anything more dreadful,' writes Grimm, who was present; and Marmontel, another guest, after a night's rest, was still tremulously under the spell. 'If we had actors like you,' he told Garrick next day, 'our scenes would not be so diffuse; we should let their silence speak, and it would say more than our verses.' The image of Macbeth, he declared, would be for him 'the intellectual model of theatrical declamation at its highest point of energy and truth'; and he seems to imply that he should utilise his memories for a study of 'Declamation' in the 'Encyclopédie.' But the intention must have faded with the impression, for the article contains no mention of Garrick.

Lapses of this sort are not unusual in light and mercurial natures; and even Garrick himself has been accused of forgetting some of his former French associates of fourteen years earlier. Collé, in particular, bitterly resented what he regarded as the difference between the 'bon enfant' of 1751 and the pampered favourite of the philosophes whom he met again in 1765. But this complaint, as M. Hedgcock points out, is an isolated one, and there are numerous instances to prove that Garrick by no means neglected his French friends. He celebrated the success of his former prognostications respecting Mlle. Clairon with an engraving after a drawing by Gravelot entitled 'La Prophétie Accomplie,' where Melpomene is represented crowning the actress, and to which is appended a quatrain by himself:

> J'ai prédit que Clairon illustrerait la scène,
> Et mon espoir n'a point été déçu;
> Elle a couronné Melpomène,
> Melpomène lui rend ce qu'elle en a reçu.

If it be replied, that Clairon was a far more important figure than the author of 'La Vérité dans le Vin,' 'who was diverted with everything, and laughed at nothing;' it may be added that Garrick certainly did not forget Monnet. When Monnet publishes a book, Garrick gets Becket to take a hundred copies; when Monnet has losses, Garrick offers him his purse; when he comes to London, Garrick places both the Thames villa and the Southampton Street house at Monnet's disposal, carries him to Bath, and sends him, jubilant, on his way. Ingratitude should be made of sterner stuff; and probably Garrick did not greatly care for Collé, who, moreover, grew with age intolerably cross-grained. His correspondence with Monnet ceased only with life. Garrick died on 20th January, 1779; and Monnet's last letter in the Forster collection is dated 4th December, 1778. It refers to the then recent deaths of Voltaire and Rousseau—of the comedian Bellecour and the tragedian Le Kain. 'We learn,' says the same letter, 'by our public prints that one of your compatriots has put an end to the Vicomte Du Barry with a pistol shot. If the race of the last had been exterminated ten years ago, France would be better, and Louis XV would be still alive.' But *that* surely was not a consummation to be wished!

Garrick returned to England in April 1765, and never revisited France. In the closing chapter M. Hedgcock devotes some pages to the actor's foreign correspondence, much of which is most interesting. D'Holbach writes of Walpole's sham letter from Frederick the Great to Voltaire, and of Sedaine's recent 'Philosophe sans le Savoir'; Chastellux expatiates on the beauty of Hampton and its weeping willow; Beaumarchais acknowledges hints for the 'Barber of Seville,' and Suard and de la Place deal with themes theatrical and literary. But, for the present, our limits are reached. M. Hedgcock, referring to Garrick's protracted stay in Paris, endeavours to account for his extraordinary popularity—a popularity which no English contemporary, Hume and Sterne not excepted, had enjoyed in like measure, and of which the echoes and memories survived long after his leaving the country. That Garrick possessed many delightful social qualities specially grateful to Frenchmen—'Il était fait pour vivre parmi nous,' they were accustomed to say—is something: that, in a mimetic nation he was a superlative master of what Scott calls 'gestic art,' is something more. But the main reason is probably that here suggested. He represented at its highest the school of natural acting which the influence of the English stage and the English novel was gradually substituting on French boards for the hide-bound formalities of the old théâtre classique. He stood for truth against tradition—for the emancipating and innovating drame sérieux of Diderot as opposed to the rigid and retrograde tragédie of Voltaire; and in these respects he supplied an object lesson at once opportune and overpowering. There may have been—nay, there cannot fail to have been—other contributing causes for his success; but, in that success, this at any rate must have played a considerable part.

LOUTHERBOURG, R.A.

ON the left bank of the Thames at Hammersmith, about halfway between Chiswick Church and the north end of Hammersmith Bridge, stand some dozen old-fashioned houses, turning their backs to the river, and known as Hammersmith Terrace. According to Faulkner, they were built 'about the year 1770,' but they were undoubtedly inhabited in the last quarter of the eighteenth century; and instead of being crowded around, as at present, by structures of all sorts, must, at that date, have looked uninterruptedly over open fields or market-gardens towards the high road from Brentford to Kensington. To the indifferent spectator they say nothing; but with a little goodwill, it is not difficult to detect in them a certain air of faded distinction which seems to shrink vaguely from vulgar encroachment. Moreover, the neighbourhood is not without its associations. Hard by, in the Upper Mall, once dwelt Catherine of Braganza, until she quitted this country for Portugal, to find her final resting place at Belem; farther

LOUTHERBOURG

(FROM THE PORTRAIT BY GAINSBOROUGH IN THE DULWICH GALLERY)

away, in Chiswick Churchyard, Hogarth lies buried. On one side are the 'new Buildings' (Mawson's Row) in which Pope translated the 'Iliad'; on the other is the Doves Tavern, where (or in the adjoining cottage once forming part of it) Thomson, according to a time-honoured tradition, worked upon his 'Winter.' The old Terrace, too, has its personal and particular memories. At No. 5 was the residence of that whilom idol of Sadler's Wells and Covent Garden, Mrs. Mountain; at No. 15 (the 'westernmost house') lived the biographer of Garrick, Arthur Murphy, the 'Mur.' of Dr. Johnson's compressed code of endearment; and at Nos. 7 and 8, for more than a quarter of a century, the artist and enthusiast, Philip de Loutherbourg. With this last we are here immediately concerned. Nothing very precise is known about him; and it is probable that he must always be more of a name than a person. Yet, in the absence of readily accessible information, he has certainly been too unceremoniously dismissed. In religion, he has been described as a 'charlatan'; in art, he has been bracketed with Zuccarelli as an 'artificial painter of so-called landscape.' Both of these characterizations do him demonstrable injustice.

Philip James de Loutherbourg, or Loutherbourgh, sometimes called the Younger, was long supposed to have been born at Strasburg. But that 'Old Mortality' of letters, the indefatigable M. Jal, ascertained definitely that his real place of nativity was Fulda in Hesse-Nassau. Here, on 31st October, 1740, he entered the world. His father, a Pole of noble extraction, was a miniaturist. He was court-painter at Darmstadt, and intended his son to become an engineer. The boy's mother (born Catherine Barbe Heitz) desired, on the contrary, to make him a Lutheran pastor, to which end he was educated at the College of Strasburg. But his personal bent was to art; and, after some preliminary tuition from his father and the elder Tischbein, he came to Paris in his teens to study under Carle Vanloo, from whose atelier he passed to that of the battle-painter François Casanova, a clever but indolent and erratic younger brother of the notorious Jacques Casanova de Seingalt, some of whose more reputable adventures are woven into the pages of Thackeray's 'Barry Lyndon.' With Casanova, Loutherbourg remained several years, since, from a remark of Diderot, who apparently knew him personally, he must have been domiciled with his master as early as 1758 or 1759. So rapid was his progress that (again according to

Diderot) he was soon qualified to render substantial aid to Casanova by finishing up his pictures, a task he performed to such good purpose, that when, about 1762, his pupilage came to an end, the absence of his handiwork from Casanova's canvases was unmistakable. Later, in 1763, Casanova, becoming an Academician, exhibited his reception-piece, a 'Combat of Cavalry'; and Loutherbourg, then not more than two and twenty, made his début with a large number of contributions, four of which, the 'Hours of the Day,' he afterwards engraved, and it is notable, looking to his latest performances, that there are ships in all of them. Unfortunately, Diderot, in his 'Salon' of 1763, confines himself to rhapsodizing over one only of Loutherbourg's performances, a 'forest scene,' which he does not name more explicitly. But his commendations of this have all the Diderot exuberance. He extols the breadth, the harmony, the excellent animal-painting of this youthful prodigy, who, at a bound, had raised himself to the level of Nicolas Berchem; and, it was whispered, surpassed his preceptor, Casanova, in his own special field. For one of Loutherbourg's exhibits—hung craftily between two restful landscapes—was a most spirited little battle-piece, signed largely 'Loutherbourg' on the frame—'as if (writes Diderot) the artist had said to all the world: "Gentlemen, recall those efforts of Casanova which so much astonished you two years ago;[1] look closely at this, and decide to whom belongs the credit of the others!"'[2]

Before the next exhibition had come round, Loutherbourg married. Beyond the facts that the marriage took place on 10th January 1764; that the name of the lady, probably an Alsatian, was Barbe Burlât; that she was a widow of five-and-twenty, and that, in due time, she bore him six children, we know nothing with certainty. Diderot, indeed, speaks of Mme. Loutherbourg as a 'compagne charmante,' but this is a mere banality. It is clear, however, that her husband was industrious; that he wrought rapidly, and found willing purchasers. He sent a number of paintings to the exhibition of 1765, 'many of which,' says his critic, 'were excellent, and none without some merit.' It is significant that the piece least commended, a 'Rendez-vous de Chasse' of the Prince de Condé in the Forest of Chantilly, was

[1] At this date, the exhibitions of the French Academy were biennial.

[2] Assézat's 'Œuvres de Diderot,' x, 200. In his later 'Salons,' Diderot qualified this opinion, and gave greater praise to Casanova.

a commission. In Diderot's words, 'the site and the subject were prescribed, and the Muse of the painter imprisoned.' In August 1767, Loutherbourg, although under age, was made an Academician, his diploma-work being a 'Combat sur Terre.' Battles, sea-pieces and storms, landscapes, and drawings made up the remainder of his contributions, eighteen in all. Diderot is still laudatory, but he notes one characteristic, which might be anticipated by those who have already remarked the painter's fertility. Loutherbourg works too much in the studio. Exceptional as his talent is, 'although he has seen much of Nature, it is not "chez elle"; it is in visits to Berchem, Wouverman, and Joseph Vernet.' The same criticism recurs in the 'Salon' of 1769, where it is also implied that prolific production is bringing about its ordinary results, monotony and repetition; and that the semblance of vigour is dearly bought by over-emphasis, in which connection a partiality for too-green fields and too-red sunsets is becoming pronounced. Of this tendency, noticed later by Horace Walpole and the remorseless 'Peter Pindar,' Diderot says elsewhere: 'There is one of these pictures by Loutherbourg where the sun is so fervid, so hot on the horizon, that it is more like a conflagration than a sunset, and one is tempted to cry to its sitting shepherdess: "Run, if you don't want to be burned."' This comes from the 'Salon' of 1771. In commending a painting in the previous exhibition, Diderot had also reverted to the need of out-door study, ending his praise with a regretful: 'Ah! si jamais cet artiste voyage et qu'il se détermine à voir la nature!'

Diderot's utterance belongs to 1769, and those who have written of Loutherbourg concur in saying that he *did* travel—in Switzerland, Germany, Italy. Whether this took place subsequent to, and in consequence of, his critic's counsel must be matter of conjecture; and after 1771 Diderot never again had the opportunity of sitting in judgement upon his work. For from that year Loutherbourg belongs to England, whither he came as a man of thirty, 'uniquement pour son plaisir,' says one account, and according to another, 'dans l'espérance d'y trouver de l'occupation, et d'y remplir ses poches de guinées,'[1] which is probably nearer the mark. In this country, with occasional visits to the Continent, he continued to reside, a naturalized subject, until his death, forty years afterwards. He lodged first in Great Marlborough Street, having for companion

[1] Mariette, 'Abecedario.'

a French enameller named Pascet who had accompanied him to London; and in 1772, he sent several contributions from this address to the Royal Academy. Over and above his artistic gifts, he had considerable mechanical aptitude; and already in France his inventive faculty had been exercised in the development of pictorial effects and stage appliances. He had devised cunning expedients for simulating sunlight and starlight, and the appearance of running water. It was natural that, in England, he should seek to open relations with the enterprising manager of Drury Lane, who was also keenly interested in improving theatrical decoration; and for this purpose he had come provided with an introduction from Garrick's French friend, Jean Monnet of the Opéra Comique,[1] who styles him 'un de nos plus grands peintres.' In the Garrick Correspondence at South Kensington there are two unpublished documents which show the progress of the intercourse thus initiated. Neither of the papers is dated; and both suggest that the painter, as regards style, was more German than French.

[1] Hedgcock's 'David Garrick et ses Amis Français,' 1911, p. 223*n*. Angelo says ('Reminiscences,' 1830, i, 265; ii, 326) that his father introduced Loutherbourg to Garrick; but the statements are not necessarily inconsistent.

From what is apparently the earlier, it must be inferred that Loutherbourg had made to Garrick certain suggestions which Garrick had requested him to put into writing. He is ready, he says, with a proposition, which should profit them both, for redecorating Drury Lane. It will of necessity involve fresh methods of lighting and scene-shifting, and new machinery. For all this he will prepare a working model to guide the artists, artificers and machinists concerned. He will design and colour all the costumes, and co-operate with the composer and 'maître-de-ballets' in such a way as to ensure harmony of action. He will also provide a trustworthy scene-painter to execute his designs, which, if need be, he will personally retouch.[1] Garrick is to pay all expenses; and he himself, for his three months labour and trouble, is to have a modest honorarium of £300.

His scheme, it will be seen, was very general in terms; and, without knowledge of the writer's

[1] This is confirmed by Angelo, who says: 'It was conditioned that De Loutherbourg should do nothing more than design the scenes, which were painted from his small, coloured sketches under his superintendence, by the scene-painters already on the theatrical establishment. I have often seen him at his easel composing these pictorial prototypes' ('Reminiscences,' 1830, i, 16).

previous communications to Garrick, not particularly easy to comprehend. But, from its reference to a specific though otherwise unspecified 'piece,' it is not unreasonable to connect it with the 'Christmas Tale,' an indifferent 'dramatic entertainment' based on Charles Favart's 'Fée Urgéle,' which Garrick 'by His Majesty's Command,' brought out at Drury Lane on Monday, 27th December 1773, with 'new Scenes, Dresses, Music, Machinery, and Decorations.' Although its purpose was 'to promote Virtue,' it had little literary merit; and if Garrick were its author, proved, as Walpole said, how poor a figure a great actor may make as a writer.[1] The music was by Dibdin; the scenery 'invented by Mr. De Loutherbourg.' As this involved a thunderstorm, a palace in flames, a 'richly illuminated cloud,' a magnificent seraglio, a rising sun and a rising moon, it is obvious that the artist must have been thoroughly at home; and it may be concluded that his efforts gave novelty and vogue to what otherwise would probably have been a very tame performance. Some-

[1] Transcripts of the 'Christmas Tale,' and its predecessor, 'Cymon' (1767), with passages in Garrick's handwriting, recently (1912) figured in a Catalogue of Mr. Bertram Dobell of Charing Cross Road.

thing, however, must have been due to the acting of Weston, the inimitable 'Scrub' of the 'Beaux' Stratagem,' who, as 'squire to the good magician, Bonoro, had an excellent Low Comedy character, which 'kept the audience in a Horse Laugh all the Time he was on the Stage'; and the published play (1774) has an etching of him by Loutherbourg, who also contributed Weston's portrait to the Pall Mall Exhibition of the same year. But, for our purpose, the essential outcome of 'A Christmas Tale' was that Loutherbourg made further overtures to Garrick.

These are embodied in a second and more lengthy document at South Kensington, headed 'Propositions de Mr. Philippe Jacque de Loutherbourg Peintre du Roy de france et membre de Son Accademie Royalle de Peinture & Sculpture aux Messieurs Garrick & L[acy] propriétaires du Spectacle de Drury lâne à Londres.' They are decidedly verbose, and, in any case, too detailed for more than a summary. Beginning with a reference to the proof of the writer's ability which he has already given (to wit, in the 'Christmas Tale'), he goes on to a particular account of what he is further disposed to do for Drury Lane—and Drury Lane exclusively—in order to place it in the first rank as regards the congruity of its costumes and appointments with the subjects of its pieces. He desires to take entire charge of the decorations, including the inventing, lighting and working of them. He will, when necessary, design suitable dresses; will provide, every winter, new effects for a piece to be concerted beforehand with the managers; and will, moreover, make sure that all arrangements for the winter season are ready betimes. As regards what the late Anthony Trollope used to call the 'interesting financial details,' he is prepared, for all this, to accept an annual payment, in monthly instalments, of six hundred guineas, being no more, his correspondents are given to understand, than Panini's pupil Servandoni had received at the Opera-house in the Haymarket for the winter season alone.

On this last point of payment, there must have been compromise, for it is admitted that his salary was settled at five hundred a year, a larger sum than Garrick had ever paid before. That the new superintendent of scenery and machinery performed his duties efficiently, there can be little doubt. He made many valuable alterations in the illumination of the stage, then very inadequate, for even sunk footlights, with their 'ineffectual fires,' were of comparatively recent date;[1] and by employing coloured silks in the flies, which turned on a pivot, and behind which lights were placed, he managed to obtain the most wonderful transitions. He got rid of the old stationary background; and by a skilful use of perspective contrived to give a better idea of distance. He is also credited with originating the 'set-scene' or built-up picture—though perhaps 'originating' should rather be 'developing' or 'elaborating.' He strove to end the glaring anachronisms of costume which Hogarth had ridiculed in the plates to the 'Analysis'; and which, in tragedy, permitted Mrs. Pritchard to play Lady Macbeth in a hoop-petticoat, perched the lacquered helmet of Alexander on an elegant Ramillies wig, and attired Othello (blackened to order) in the laced red coat of King William's 'Gentlemen of the Guard.'[2] But of these things the chronicle is scant and dispersed; and we can

[1] Besant's 'London in the Eighteenth Century,' 1902, 431.

[2] 'Wine and Walnuts,' by 'Ephraim Hardcastle' (W. H. Pyne, the painter and etcher), 2nd ed. 1824, i, 279. These irregularities must, nevertheless, have died hard, for, according to Mangin's 'Parlour Window,' 1841, p. 123, John Kemble still fought Bosworth Field in silk stockings and dancing shoes, and played Lear or Macbeth in a Louis-Quinze nightgown of flowered satin.

here do no more than pick out, from the public prints and elsewhere, a few of the pieces with which he seems to have been intimately concerned.

In 1774 he helped to bolster up Burgoyne's mediocre 'dramatic entertainment,' the 'Maid of the Oaks,'[1] and in the two following years lent effective aid both to Bickerstaffe's 'Sultan' and Collier's Persian Tale of 'Selima and Azor.' In 1776 he is also credited by the 'Morning Chronicle' with 'a very beautiful scene' of the Pantheon at Spa Fields for Colman's farce of 'The Spleen'[2] in the Prologue to which Garrick gave the first public intimation of his approaching retirement; and the late Sir Henry Irving had

[1] First acted at 'The Oaks,' Epsom, on the marriage of Burgoyne's nephew, Lord Stanley, to Lady Betty Hamilton. Both Walpole and Hannah More mention this piece. It is 'as fine as scenes can make it,' says Horace to Conway in Nov. 1774, 'and as dull as the author could not help making it.' St. Hannah is kinder. 'The scenery is beautiful—the masquerade scene as good as at the Pantheon. The piece is only intended as a vehicle for the scenery; yet there is some wit and spirit in it, being written by General Burgoyne, and embellished, etc., by Garrick' ('Memoirs,' 1834, i, 39). Loutherbourg was referred to in it as 'Mr. Lanternbug'—which his artist friends corrupted into 'Leatherbag.'

[2] Loutherbourg painted a portrait of Colman, of which there is a print by Cheesman.

several sketches which Loutherbourg had prepared for the final performances of 'Richard III.' When, later, Drury Lane passed to Sheridan, Loutherbourg for a brief period retained his office, painting, according to Baker and Reed, who styled him 'the first scene painter in Europe,' an excellent representation of Cox Heath, near Maidstone, for Linley's 'Camp' (1778); and for the 'Critic' of 1779, another of Tilbury Fort, which procured his inclusion in the 'puff direct' of that piece. 'The miraculous powers of Mr. de Loutherbourg's pencil are universally acknowledged,' says this panegyrist. He also contributed to keep alive the insipid pantomime of 'Robinson Crusoe; or, Harlequin Friday,' which Sheridan patched together for 1781. After this, it was ungratefully proposed to reduce his salary by half, an arrangement which he indignantly refused to accept. His last stage-work seems to have been in connection with O'Keeffe's 'Omai; or, A Trip round the World,' produced at Covent Garden in 1785, the decorations of which are directly attributed to him by the authors of the 'Biographia Dramatica.' Omai, or Omiah, who gives his name to the piece, was an Otaheitan, brought ten years earlier from the Society Islands, on Cook's second voyage, by Fanny

Burney's brother James; and, in designing appropriate costumes, Loutherbourg had the assistance of sketches made by John Webber, the landscape painter, and draughtsman of the expedition. He got £100 for his services, which must have afforded him ample opportunity for volcanoes and other congenial phenomena. The performance closed with an apotheosis of the great circumnavigator, which was afterwards engraved. 'Omai' ran forty nights; and, we are told, was frequently 'commanded by Their Majesties.'

But this is to anticipate. In 1774 Loutherbourg had moved to 45, Great Titchfield Street, Oxford Market, where one of his later neighbours was to be Richard Wilson, another landscapist whose works lay under the imputation of being 'screeny,' that is, 'stagey,' in character. During the period of Loutherbourg's connection with Garrick he had gone on exhibiting annually at the Royal Academy in his former manner—landscapes with cattle, mornings, evenings, banditti, and the like. 'We have a Swede [German],' says Walpole in April 1775, 'one Loutherbourg, who would paint landscape and cattle excellently if he did not in every picture indulge some one colour inordinately.'[1] This, as the reader will

[1] Wright, in his life of Wilson (1824), while speaking

observe, had been one of the objections of Diderot; and it was heavily underlined a little later by 'Peter Pindar' in his 'Odes to the Royal Academicians" of 1782:

> And, *Loutherbourg*, when Heav'n so wills,
> To make brass skies and golden hills,
> With marble bullocks in glass pastures grazing,
> Thy reputation too will rise,
> And people, gaping with surprise,
> Cry 'Monsieur *Loutherbourgh* is most amazing!'

He diversified his contributions by an occasional portrait, one of which was of course that popular impersonation, 'Roscius' as 'Richard III.' His only military compositions were two representing a review and manœuvres at Warley Camp in 1778. (Lovers of Boswell may be reminded that Dr. Johnson came to Warley in this very year, on a visit to Bennet Langton, then doing duty as an officer of the Lincolnshire Militia, on which occasion the great man made minute inquisition into the weight of musket balls; and was highly

of Loutherbourg as scarcely ever surpassed in execution, refers to the 'very glaring and oftentimes unharmonious tints' his pictures displayed, as 'unaccountable in an artist of so much practice and experience, and who, in many respects, was certainly a delightful painter' (p. 153).

impressed by the dexterity with which the Corporal Trim of the period handled his 'Brown Bess.') It may have been these last productions which, in 1780, procured for Loutherbourg his associateship; and in 1781, when he exhibited nothing, the further distinction of R.A. At this date his leisure must have been employed in projecting and perfecting that curious product of his combined ingenuities as scene-painter and machinist, the 'EIDOPHUSIKON; or, Various Imitations of Natural Phenomena, represented by Moving Pictures.'

From some of the accounts of this long-vanished exhibition, it might easily be concluded that it was little more than an elaboration of those pictorial 'Waterworks' at Vauxhall which Goldsmith's pawnbroker's widow did *not* see, when, under the experienced guidance of Mr. and Mrs. Tibbs, she visited the Surrey gardens for that special purpose. But this is to rate Loutherbourg's performance far too low. It was a really clever and novel attempt by an artist of very varied equipment to represent landscape and locality as subjected to all the changes of light and darkness, time and season, heat and cold. Its first home, in 1781-2, was a large house in Lisle Street, fronting Leicester Street, Leicester

Square. But in the early months of 1786, when described by Pyne,[1] it was located in Old Exeter 'Change, Strand, where the body of John Gay had once lain in state. Here it occupied an upper floor previously used for Dibdin and Stoppelaer's puppet Patagonian Theatre and afterwards given over to those wild beasts whose hungry roarings, in Leigh Hunt's day, terrified the horses in the Strand. During Loutherbourg's tenancy, the place was arranged by Bateman as a tiny theatre, with a stage about six feet wide and eight feet deep. But Pyne, as a professing eye-witness, may now be quoted:

'The opening subject of the Eidophusikon represented the view from the summit of One-Tree Hill, in Greenwich Park, looking up the Thames to the metropolis; on one side, conspicuous upon its picturesque eminence, stood Flamsteed House [the Observatory]; and below, on the right, the grand mass of building, Greenwich Hospital, with its imposing cupolas, cut out of pasteboard, and painted with architectural correctness. The large groups of trees formed another division, behind which were the towns of Greenwich and Deptford, with the shore on each side stretching to the metropolis, which was

[1] 'Wine and Walnuts,' 2nd ed. 1824, i, ch. xxi.

seen in its vast extent from Chelsea to Poplar. Behind were the hills of Hampstead, Highgate, and Harrow; and the intermediate space was occupied by the flat stage, as the pool or port of London, crowded with shipping, each mass of which being cut out in pasteboard, and receding in size by the perspective of their distance. The heathy appearance of the foreground was constructed of cork, broken into the rugged and picturesque form of a sand-pit[1] covered with minute mosses and lichens, producing a captivating effect, amounting indeed to reality.

'This scene, on the rising of the curtain, was enveloped in that mysterious light which is the precursor of day-break, so true to nature, that the imagination of the spectator sniffed the sweet breath of morn. A faint light appeared along the horizon; the scene assumed a vapourish tint of grey; presently a gleam of saffron, changing to the pure varieties that tinge the fleecy clouds that pass away in morning mist; the picture brightened by degrees; the sun appeared, gilding the tops of the trees and the projections of the lofty buildings, and burnishing the vanes on the cupolas; when the whole scene burst upon the

[1] One of Loutherbourg's exhibits of 1782 was 'A Sand-Pit.'

eye in the gorgeous splendour of a beauteous day.'

At this time gas was not in use, and Loutherbourg's illuminating power was restricted to a brilliant row of the then newly introduced Argand lamps, which lighted the stage from above. It would take too long to describe the ingenious contrivances by which the artist obtained his various effects: the stained glass that altered the colouring of his scene; the expedients for imitating thunder and lightning, hail and rain, the changes of cloud-form, the tumbling of waves, the sound of signal-guns at sea. One of his most striking tableaux reproduced the loss, with all its appalling circumstance, off the coast of Dorset, on the 6th January 1786, of the 'Halsewell' East Indiaman,[1] so feelingly sung in 'Lewesdon Hill' by Rogers's Miltonic friend, William Crowe; and the representation was realistic enough to satisfy even the most exacting nautical critics. The finale travelled beyond sublunary judgment, for it exhibited 'the region of the fallen angels, with Satan arraying his troops on the banks of

[1] This 'late dreadful Catastrophe,' according to the advertisements in the newspapers of the day, was one of the reasons for reviving the Eidophusikon at the beginning of 1786.

the Fiery Lake,' and also the uprising of that Palace of Pandemonium described in the first book of 'Paradise Lost':

> Anon out of the earth a Fabrick huge
> Rose like an Exhalation, with the sound
> Of Dulcet Symphonies and voices sweet,
> Built like a Temple, where *Pilasters* round
> Were set, and Doric pillars overlaid
> With Golden Architrave; nor did there want
> Cornice or Freeze, with bossy Sculptures grav'n,
> The roof was fretted gold.

Here, from Pyne, is the pictorial materialization of the lines; and it will be seen that the subject elicited all Loutherbourg's faculty for lurid effects: 'In the foreground of a vista, stretching an immeasurable length between mountains, ignited from their bases to their lofty summits, with many coloured flame, a chaotic mass rose in dark majesty, which gradually assumed form until it stood, the interior of a vast temple of gorgeous architecture, bright as molten brass, seemingly composed of unconsuming and unquenchable fire. In this tremendous scene, the effect of coloured glasses before the lamps was fully displayed; which, being hidden from the audience, threw their whole influence upon the scene, as it rapidly changed, now to a sulphurous blue, then to a lurid red, and then again to a pale vivid light, and ultimately to a mysterious combination of the glasses, such as a bright furnace exhibits, in-fusing various metals.'

During the last phases of this manifestation, we are told, resounding peals of thunder added a preternatural horror, heightened by 'a variety of groans, that struck the imagination as issuing from infernal spirits.' For those accustomed to the cinematograph and the elaborate combinations of modern stage machinery, such an exhibition may well seem primitive and rudimentary; but it was not so to Loutherbourg's public; and a convincing proof of the fidelity of the above description lies in the fact that the most devoted admirers of the Eidophusikon were its inventor's most distinguished brethren of the brush. Reynolds praised it warmly, and recommended all his friends to take their daughters to see it; while Gainsborough, who for some time spent his evenings there, could talk of nothing else.[1] Between

[1] He even made a toy Eidophusikon or peep-show box for himself, which was shown at the Grosvenor Gallery in 1885. It then belonged to Mr. G. W. Reid, its former possessor having been Dr. Monro. The slides were painted on glass, were lighted from behind, and looked at through a magnifier ('Somerset House Gazette,' 1824, ii, pp. 8, 11).

the scenes, it should be added, there was, at the outset, music and singing, a feature of the entertainment which led to Loutherbourg's being summoned for purveying unlicensed harmony. But the sitting justices showed their sense of the triviality of the charge by forthwith granting the required permit without penalty, and for a space the show continued to prosper. Like most other things, however, it had its day; and when at last it was disposed of by its projector, the door-money had fallen so low as to be insufficient to cover the lighting expenses.[1]

By 1783 Loutherbourg had moved from Titchfield Street to Prince's Street, Hammersmith; and two years later he was in residence at Hammersmith Terrace. At this date he seems to have temporarily abandoned the old studio-pictures on the model of Berchem and Wouverman, and devoted his attention to the natural scenery of his adopted country. 'No English landscape painter,' he is reported to have said, 'needed foreign travel to collect grand prototypes for his study.' His own contributions to the Academy for the next few years prove that he paid repeated visits to the Lakes, to York-

[1] See, for further details, Appendix B (Exhibitions of the Eidophusikon).

shire, Derbyshire[1] and Wales. He must also have visited Switzerland, for his solitary exhibit in 1788 was a view of the Grand Cataract of the Rhine at Schaffhausen. In 1789 he sent nothing; and with this defection is connected a curious and rather unexpected episode in his career. After settling down permanently at Hammersmith, his restless energies seem to have involved him in that cloud of occultism which brooded heavily over revolutionary Europe in the last quarter of the eighteenth century. He grew interested in Mesmer's Animal Magnetism; and became a pupil of the Dr. de Mainauduc whose 'demoniacal mummery' fluttered the pious apprehensions of Hannah More. He is also said to have travelled in Switzerland with the Sicilian impostor and mountebank, Giuseppe Balsamo, otherwise Cagliostro, whom he may have met in Strasburg in 1783, where His Quackship was dosing, among others, Gibbon's friend Deyverdun.[2] Or he may have made his acquaintance

[1] He had already visited Derbyshire previous to 1779, when he utilized his experiences for the Drury Lane pantomime 'The Wonders of Derbyshire.

[2] 'On ne sait qui il est, d'où il est, d'où il tire son argent; il exerce gratis ses talens pour la médicine; il a fait des cures admirables; mais c'est d'ailleurs le composé le plus étrange.

on one of his visits to England—notably that final sojourn when Cagliostro, after the Necklace Scandal, resided here in 1786-7, leaving his wife, on his departure, in the temporary charge of the Loutherbourgs. In any case, it should have been Cagliostro who set Loutherbourg on the search for the philosopher's stone, an enterprise which he pursued assiduously until an exasperated female relative, not otherwise identified, ruthlessly wrecked his crucibles—of course at the critical moment of projection. Later he persuaded himself that he possessed supernatural healing powers. A room in his house was set apart for patients, and special days were advertised for their attendance. 'Loutherbourg, the painter,' says Horace Walpole to Lady Ossory in July 1789, 'is turned an inspired physician, and has three thousand patients. His sovereign panacea is barley-water. I believe it is as efficacious as mesmerism.' A more material testimony to Loutherbourg's doings is supplied by a nine-page quarto pamphlet on the subject, written by one Mary Pratt, of No. 41, Portland Street, Marylebone, described as a 'lady of deep and original

J'ai cessé de prendre ses remèdes qui m'échauffaient—l'homme d'ailleurs me gâtoit le médecin.' ('Deyverdun to Gibbon,' [June 1783].)

piety.' It was published in 1789; is dedicated to the Archbishop of Canterbury, and is entitled, 'A List of a few Cures performed by Mr. and Mrs. De Loutherbourg, of Hammersmith Terrace, without Medicine.' Mrs. De Loutherbourg (a second wife),[1] participated, as will be seen, in her husband's gift, and, for a time, patients, 'deaf, dumb, lame, halt, and blind,' crowded to the free ministrations of the consulting room, while, in the public prints, 'Amicus' and 'Fame' hotly discussed the validity of the results. Then came the inevitable reaction. Something went wrong; and the fickle mob proceeded to smash the windows of the hapless philanthropists, who, for a season, had to retire 'into the country,' and the 'Public Advertiser' announced that 'the Magnetising Doctor of Hammersmith had given over practice.'

After this, we hear no more of Loutherbourg's 'wonder-working,' though it is not unlikely that he continued to dabble in medicine, since, from a letter we have seen, even as late as 1803, he was still preoccupied with diet-drinks. And he must always have been mixed up with visionaries of some sort. One of his associates, later a resid-

[1] Angelo says she was a beautiful widow named Smith ('Reminiscences,' 1830, ii, 330).

ent of Chiswick, was the engraver-enthusiast, William Sharp, a Swedenborgian, and the republican friend of Tom Paine and Horne Tooke. Sharp was also a devotee of the self-styled 'Prince of the Hebrews' and 'prophet,' Richard Brothers, whose portrait he engraved, appending to it a signed inscription expressing full belief in his mission and powers. Brothers, in 1795, went so far as to predict the death of George the Third, an unfortunate vaticination which, coupled with his personal pretensions to the succession, led to his incarceration as a treasonable lunatic. It is sometimes alleged that his influence brought about the disclosure of the painter's alleged curative gift. But Brothers, a retired lieutenant in the navy, who had been present in 1782 at the famous action between Rodney and de Grasse, did not receive his prophetical 'call' until a much later period; and the Hammersmith healing-room belongs demonstrably to 1789, since Mrs. Pratt's pamphlet is dated July in that year, and covers the previous six months. The whole of this part of Loutherbourg's biography is nevertheless obscure. Its connection with his art-life is purely incidental; and one turns willingly to the story of his pictures, pausing only to note that there is no reason to suppose he was insincere, a circumstance which should of itself suffice to absolve him from any charge of charlatanry.

For the next few years he reverted to his former fashion of studio-landscapes. Then, in 1793, came the tragedy of Louis XVI, and France's declaration of war with England. Loutherbourg's efforts at Warley Camp were no doubt remembered; and at the opening of the campaign he was despatched to Flanders, with Gillray the caricaturist, to make graphic celebration of the anticipated exploits of that not-too-distinguished commander, King George's soldier son, the Duke of York. At what particular sieges Loutherbourg assisted does not appear, but he certainly painted the Grand Attack on Valenciennes in July, for it was engraved by Bromley. In the following June (1794), when Howe's success in the Brest waters served, to some extent, as a set-off to the land triumphs of the French at Tournay and elsewhere, Loutherbourg was commissioned to prepare a companion canvas commemorating the opening encounter of the rival flagships, the 'Queen Charlotte' and the 'Montagne.' He must have executed his task with his usual rapidity, for in March of the next year both pictures were exhibited at the Historic Gallery in Pall Mall. James Fittler, the King's marine engraver, made a fine print of the 'glorious victory'; and the original is still to be seen in the Painted Hall at Greenwich Hospital,[1] to which, by the gift of George IV, it was transferred from St. James's Palace. After Howe's engagement came Duncan's great battle off Camperdown with De Winter, which besides preventing the invasion of Ireland by the Dutch, provided a fresh subject for Loutherbourg's pencil. In the Print Room at the British Museum, carefully catalogued by Mr. Laurence Binyon, are a number of minutely finished studies and sketches for these works, particularly an album containing many plans of actions, views of localities, details of sword-hilt and ammunition-pouch, mizen-top and cat-head, flags, guns, sails, rigging, and a host of artistic 'marginalia,' which prove how little, in his marine pieces at all events, the painter relied on his imagination for his facts.

His remaining story may be abridged. He

[1] In the Painted Hall is another of Loutherbourg's efforts, 'The Defeat of the Spanish Armada,' which was presented to the Hospital by Lord Farnborough, and has been called 'one of the finest sea-fights ever realized on canvas.' This, like the Stratton 'Great Fire of London,' was doubtless executed for Bowyer's 'History of England.' 'The Attack on Valenciennes' is in the Royal collection.

painted the 'Battle of the Nile' (1798), familiar in Fittler's engraving. He continued to exhibit at the Royal Academy, somewhat irregularly, until his death, two of his most important efforts being the 'Landing of the British Troops at Aboukir Bay,' and the 'Battle of Alexandria,' both of which events belong to March 1801, although the pictures were not shown until later. In 1801 and 1805 were issued two large volumes of 'Romantic and Picturesque Scenery in England and Wales,' containing a series of coloured plates after his paintings. To Macklin's great seven-volume Bible, besides many head and tail-pieces, he contributed the 'Universal Deluge' and the 'Destruction of the Assyrian Host,' the former of which is by many regarded as his chef-d'œuvre. He was also employed as an illustrator on Bowyer's 'History of England,' Bell's 'British Theatre,' and other publications. Examples of his work are not common; but besides those at Greenwich Hospital there are specimens in the National Gallery, the Tate Gallery, the Glasgow Gallery, and at South Kensington, Vienna, and Bordeaux. He resided to the last in his house at Hammersmith, where he was well known and popular; and where he was occasionally visited by George III. Gainsborough painted his portrait, which, with two of his landscapes, is at Dulwich.[1] He died on 11th March 1812, and was buried on the 25th at the north-west end of Chiswick Churchyard, under an unattractive monument by Sir John Soane, and an inordinate epitaph by the Rev. Dr. Christopher Lake Moody, which lays special stress on his 'piety' and 'suavity of manners,' and closes with the following quatrain:

> Here, Loutherbourg, repose thy laurel'd head;
> While art is cherished thou canst ne'er be dead:
> Salvator, Poussin, Claude, thy skill combines,
> And beauteous nature lives in thy designs.

The registers also record the interment at Chiswick, in 1813 and 1828 respectively, of Salome and Lucy de Loutherbourg, his sister and his second wife.[2]

As implied at the outset, it is difficult to make of Loutherbourg that picture of the man which is often so lightly demanded by the irresponsible

[1] Sir Francis Bourgeois, R.A., the founder of the Dulwich Gallery, was a pupil of Loutherbourg. Another was De Quincey's brother.

[2] These last details were contributed by Colonel Chester in 1881 to 'Notes and Queries,' from whose indispensable and all-preserving pages we have derived some other particulars in this paper.

critic. Besides a few early and dubious 'on dits' of Diderot, an anecdote or two from Angelo, and the final statement of Faulkner that 'he was held in great esteem for the uniform propriety of his conduct,' but little exists on which to build a personality. There is, of course, the healing episode. But concerning this, fuller information is desirable; and at present the evidence is mainly confined to Mrs. Pratt's pamphlet, which was published against Loutherbourg's wishes. In dealing with Loutherbourg as an artist, however, the ground is surer, and general deductions may safely be drawn. Not to speak of his proficiency as an etcher and caricaturist, it is clear that he was a painter of unusual precocity, dexterity, and fertility of resource. Combined with these qualities was a certain constructive ingenuity which lends a special character to his productions; and moreover, served him exceptionally in his efforts as a scene-painter. On the other hand, his success as a scene-painter, since it probably increased his tendency to forced contrasts and imaginative colouring, was unfavourable to his gifts as a landscapist. Yet he could sometimes forget hot reds and vivid greens. From his 'Picturesque Scenery' it is plain that he could follow Nature closely enough when he chose to keep his eye on the object; and he possessed powers by no means to be despised. Had he lived twenty years later he might, with his mastery of technique and his assimilative talent, have figured in the forefront of the coming English landscape school. As it is, he was not without his influence on Turner.[1] And the more considerable of his great naval compositions are still justly regarded as extraordinary tours de force in their very adventurous kind.

[1] It is said that Turner first went to live in the Upper Mall at Hammersmith in 1808 in order to be near Loutherbourg (Monkhouse's 'Turner,' 1879, p. 86).

A FIELDING 'FIND'

FIELDING'S autographs and letters are admittedly few in number. 'Where,' asked an inquiring daily paper the other day, apropos of the unprecedented sale of a Fielding receipt and agreement for more than a thousand pounds —'where is the manuscript of 'Tom Jones' or of 'Amelia'? The answer is not far to seek. Probably neither now exists, since in Fielding's day authors were not so careful to preserve their 'copy' as Thackeray and Dickens and Trollope in ours. With respect to the absence of letters, there are two explanations, each of which is almost sufficient to account for their rarity. The bulk of Fielding's correspondence, it is understood, was destroyed early in the last century; and it is suggested that such of his papers as, after the sale of his library in February 1755 still remained in the custody of Sir John Fielding, his blind half-brother and successor, perished when, in 1780, the Bow Street house was wrecked by the Gordon rioters. Thus it comes about that not many specimens of Henry Fielding's epistolary efforts have been printed or preserved. Some of these are frankly formal, and consequently barren of interest; so that, with exception of one to be reproduced presently, and another to his publisher, John Nourse of the Strand, in regard to the leasing of a house near the Temple which was to include 'one large eating Parlour'[1] (a very characteristic touch!), there are practically no utterances in this kind which can be said to have any direct bearing on his biography or personality.

A fortunate circumstance has brought to light two of his latest if not his last letters, the existence of which has hitherto been overlooked; and, by the kindness of members of the Fielding family, transcripts of these have been courteously placed in our hands for publication. They relate to that voyage to Lisbon in search of health of which Fielding wrote the 'Journal' published posthumously in 1755; and they succeed and supplement the very valuable letter dating from the same period, already referred to. This has been printed in recent biographies of Fielding; but its close connection with the newly-discovered

[1] This must have been eighteenth-century for 'dining-room.' Miss Burney speaks of the 'eating-parlour' in the Queen's Lodge at Windsor ('Diary,' iv (1905), 277).

documents makes it convenient to print it once more. Fielding, it will be remembered, left Ealing for Lisbon on 26th June 1754. He was suffering from 'a complication of disorders'—asthma, jaundice, and dropsy. He had tried 'Spot' Ward's remedies and Bishop Berkeley's tar-water without permanent relief; and when finally, having made his will, he started for Portugal, he had little real hope of regaining his strength.[1] It is needless to recapitulate the trials and vexations of his protracted voyage, which are fully detailed in the 'Journal';[2] but the above-mentioned letter, it should be stated, was addressed to John Fielding Esq., at Bow Street, Covent Garden, when its writer, in the course of his travels, had reached the Isle of Wight.

'On board the Queen of Portugal, Richd Veal at anchor on the Mother Bank, off Ryde, to the care of the Post Master at Portsmouth—this is my Date and y^{r} Direction.

'*July* 12 1754.

'DEAR JACK, After receiving that agreeable Lre from Messrs Fielding and C^{o}., we weighed

[1] His death was actually announced in one of the evening papers (Godden's 'Henry Fielding,' 1910, 285).

[2] An edition, with numerous notes by the author of this paper, is included in the 'World's Classics' for 1907.

on monday morning and sailed from Deal to the Westward Four Days long but inconceivably pleasant passage brought us yesterday to an Anchor on the Mother Bank, on the Back of the Isle of Wight, where we had last Night in Safety the Pleasure of hearing the Winds roar over our Heads in as violent a Tempest as I have known, and where my only Consideration were the Fears which must possess any Friend of ours, (if there is happily any such) who really makes our Well-being the Object of his Concern especially if such Friend should be totally inexperienced in Sea Affairs. I therefore beg that on the Day you receive this Mrs. Daniel may know that we are just risen from Breakfast in Health and Spirits this twelfth Instant at 9 in the morning. Our Voyage hath proved fruitful in Adventures all which being to be written in the Book you must postpone y^r Curiosity. As the Incidents which fall under y^r Cognizance will possibly be consigned to Oblivion, do give them to us as they pass. Tell y^r Neighbour I am much obliged to him for recommending me to the care of a most able and experienced Seaman to whom other Captains seem to pay such Deference that they attend and watch his Motions, and think themselves only safe when they act under his Direction and Example. Our Ship in Truth seems to give Laws on the Water with as much Authority and Superiority as you Dispense Laws to the Public and Example to yr Brethren in Commission. Please to direct yr Answer to me on Board as in the Date, if gone to be returned, and then send it by the Post and Pacquet to Lisbon to

'Yr affect Brother

'H. FIELDING.'

This letter, apart from its manly, cheerful tone, affords a good deal of minor information. It mentions the writer's mother-in-law, Mrs. Daniel, who had probably remained at Ealing in charge of his remaining children; it gives the names of the captain and of the ship, not given in the 'Journal'; it refers to the 'Journal' itself as in progress or contemplation; and it confirms the fact that John Fielding (and not Saunders Welch, as Boswell thought) was his brother's immediate successor at Bow Street. From the Isle of Wight, the 'Queen of Portugal' proceeded to Tor Bay, whence the earlier of the two new letters is dated. It is addressed as before to John Fielding:

'TORR BAY, *July* 22, 1754.

'DEAR JACK Soon after I had concluded my Letter of Business to Welch yesterday, we came to an Anchor in this Place, which our Capt says is the best Harbour in the World. I soon remembered the Country and that it was in the midst of the South Hams a Place famous for Cyder and I think the best in England, in great Preference to that of Herefordshire. Now as I recollect that you are a Lover of this Liquor when mixed with a Proper Number of Midd^{x} Turneps, as you are of Port Wind well mixed likewise, I thought you might for the Sake of Variety be pleased with once tasting what is pure and genuine, I have therefore purchased and paid for 2 Hdds of this Cyder when they will be delivered in double Casks to y^{r} Order transmitted by any Master of a Coasting Veſſel that comes from London to these Parts. You must send the very Paper inclosed that being the Token of the Delivery. The Freight of both by a Coaster of Devon or Cornwall will be 8 shillings only, which is I believe y^{r} whole Expence. They stand me within a few shillings at 4£, and the learned here are of Opinion they are the finest of their kind, one being of the rougher the other of the sweeter Taste. Welch will easily find almost every Day one of these Coasters in London, which the Uncertainty of our Stay here and the Hurry which every Veering of the Wind puts us in prevents my providing here. It will be fit for drinking or bottling a Month after it hath lain in your Vault. I have consigned it in the following manner. Half a Hdd to yourself, half to Welch, half to Hunter and half to Millar, and I wish you all merry over it.

'In your last, there is only one Paragraph which I wish better explained. *If Boor be trusty.* Pray let me know any Shadow of a Doubt: for the very Supposition gives me much Uneasiness. If he is not trusty he is a Fool; but that is very possible for him to be, at least to catch at a leſſor, and dishonest Profit, which is present and certain in Preference to what is in all Respects its Reverse. Pray give me as perfect Ease as you can in this Particular. I begin to despair of letting my House this Summer. I hope the Sale of my Wine may be more depended on: for the almost miraculous Dilatoriness of our Voyage, tho it hath added something to the Pleasure, hath added much more to the Expense of it. In so much that I wish Welch would send a 20£ Bill of Exch[e] by [*word illegible*] means immediately after me; tho I fear Boor[s] Demands for Harvest Labourers have greatly emptied his hands, and I would not for good Reasons be too much a Debtor to the best of Friends. I hope at the same time to see a particular Account of the State of Affairs at Fordhook, and the whole Sum of Payments to Boor from my leaving him to the date of such Letter, when I presume the Harvest, as to England, will be pretty well over. I beg likewise an exact Account of the Price of Wheat p Load at Uxbridge. I have no more of Business to say, nor do I know what else to write you: for even the Winds with us afford no variety. I got half a Buck from the New Forest, while we lay at the Isle of Wight, and the Pasty still sticks by us. We have here the finest of Fish, Turbot, vast Soals and Whitings for less than you can eat Plaise in Mdd^{x}. So that Lord Cromarty^{s} Banishment from Scotland hither was somewhat less cruel than that of Ovid from Rome to Pontus.[1] We may however say with him—"Quam vicina est ultima Terra mihi!" Ultima Terra you know is the Land^{s} End which a ten Hours Gale from North or East will carry us to, and where y^{r} Health with all our Friends left behind us in England will be most cheerfully drunk by

'Y^{r} affect^{e} Brother

'H. FIELDING.

'All our loves to my sister.'

[1] This reference to Lord Cromarty is doubtless due to Fielding's connection with the anti-Jacobite press.

This very characteristic epistle is to the full as interesting, and almost as informing as that written ten days earlier from the Isle of Wight. A few sentences need brief comment. In the 'Journal' the reference to 'Middlesex Turneps' is made clear by the statement that this 'watry' vegetable entered largely into the composition of the metropolitan 'Vinum Pomonæ.'[1] The peculiar description of wine as 'wind,' was, besides being a popular vulgarism,[2] a curiosity of the Ryde landlady's little account. From the 'Journal' it also seems that Fielding purchased a third hogshead of cider for himself, which brought his expenditure up to £5 10*s*. 'Cheeshurst,' given in the printed record as the address of Mr. Giles Leverance, the salesman, should have been the name of his farm, for in the letter, or rather at the back of it, he is described in another script as of Churston, that is—Churston-Ferrers, a village on the Devon Coast near Brixham. Welch was Saun-

[1] 'But this I warn Thee, and shall alway warn,
No heterogenous Mixtures use, as some
With watry Turneps have debas'd their Wines,
Too frugal.'—(Philips' 'Cyder,' 1708, Bk. ii.)

[2] The 'fine gentleman' in 'Humphry Clinker,' it may be remembered, offers to treat Miss Winifred Jenkins with 'a pint of wind' (2nd ed., i, 231).

ders Welch, High Constable of Holborn, the friend of Johnson and Hogarth as well as of Fielding, and the father-in-law of Nollekens, the sculptor; Hunter was William Hunter, the 'great surgeon and anatomist of Covent garden'; and Millar was Andrew Millar, Fielding's publisher, of 'Shakespear's Head over-against Katherine Street in the Strand.' Boor, whose trustworthiness is under suspicion, must have been the Richard Boor who was one of the witnesses to the undated Will executed by Fielding at Ealing before his departure from England. He was also, in all likelihood, the bailiff or agent-in-charge of the 'little house' at Ealing (Fordhook),[1] which if it involved harvesting and wheat crops, should have had farm-land attached to it. The 'buck,' and the pasty which Mrs. Fielding made therefrom, are both mentioned in the 'Journal.' Lord Cromarty was George Mackenzie, the

[1] Fordhook no longer exists; and the site, on the Uxbridge Road, opposite the Ealing Common Station of the Metropolitan District Railway, is now covered by houses. A sketch of it, as somewhat altered and enlarged by subsequent occupants, is to be found in the Guildhall Library. From a plan in the Ealing Town Hall, dated 1741, there were then fields to the north and east, and later tenants seem to have held land. 'Fielding Terrace' and 'Fordhook Avenue' preserve its memory.

third earl, sentenced to death after the '45, but respited. He was allowed to reside at Layhill in Devonshire. The apposite Latin quotation which Fielding makes in this connection is a fresh instance of that natural habit of letters on his part which a cheap criticism is accustomed to stigmatize as pretentious erudition; and the lady referred to in the postscript was probably John Fielding's first wife, Elizabeth Whittingham, whose adopted daughter, Mary Ann, afterwards married the novelist's son Allen.

The seal of this document, part of which remains, displays the double-headed Austrian eagle bearing a coat-of-arms on its breast.[1] The second letter differs considerably from those which have been quoted hitherto. In the first place, it is much longer; and in places exhibits signs of haste and a perturbation of spirit which are absent from its predecessors, although now and again the old joy of life and natural cheerfulness break out irrepressibly. The writing is sometimes scarcely decipherable; and the paper in places is torn and mutilated—a condition of things which fully

[1] This shows that Fielding would probably have disapproved the modern discoveries of Mr. J. Horace Round in regard to the relations of the Denbighs and the Habsburgs.

justifies the treatment by paraphrase of part of its matter. From internal evidence it must have been written about two or three weeks after Fielding reached Lisbon on August 14. For its better comprehension, it may be well to remind the reader that Fielding's party, as expressly stated in the 'Journal,' consisted of *six* persons: namely—Fielding himself; his wife; his eldest daughter, Harriot; Mrs. Fielding's 'friend,' Miss Margaret Collier; and two servants, a footman, William, whose ignoble surname has not survived, and a maid, Isabella Ash, who, with Miss Collier and Richard Boor, had witnessed the Ealing will. Miss Collier, who was a daughter of Arthur Collier, the metaphysician and author of 'Clavis Universalis,' was doubtless well acquainted with the family, for her sister, Jane, had collaborated with Sarah Fielding in the 'New Dramatic Fable' of 'The Cry,' published by Dodsley in the March of this year. Though addressed as before to John Fielding, Esq.: 'p. the Lisbon Packet,' the letter begins without further ceremony as follows:

'I am willing to waste no Paper as you see, nor to put you to the Expense of a double Letter as I write by the Packet, by which I would have you write to me every Letter of Consequence, if it be a single Sheet of Paper only it will not cost the more for being full and perhaps you have not time even to fill one Sheet for as I take it the idlest Man in the World writes now to the busiest, and that too at the Expence of the latter.

'I have rec^{d} here two Letters from you and one from Welch. The money I have tho I was forced to discount the Note, it being drawn at 36 days Sight upon a Portugese who never doth anything for nothing. I believe as it was in Portugese neither you nor Welch knew this, and it was the Imposition of the Drawer in London. Your Letter of Business I have not yet seen. Perhaps it is lost, as if it came by a Merchant Ship it easily may: for the Captains of these Ships pay no Regard to any but Merchants for which Reason I will have all my Goods even to the smallest Parcel consigned to John Stubbs Esqr (as I mentioned before, and hope will be done long before y^{o} receive this) marked with the large red F.— Pardon Repetition for abundans Cautela non nocet, and tho I mentioned my orders, I did not give the Reason I believe either to y^{o} or Welch, at least all my Reasons for these are Several but this is most worth y^{r} Notice. The Truth is that Captains are all ye greatest Scoundrels in the World but Veale is the greatest of them all. This I did not find out till the Day before he sailed, which will explain many Things when you see him as perhaps you may for he is likewise a Madman, which I knew long before I reached Lisbon and he sailed a few Days ago. I shall not, after what I have said, think him worth my Notice, unless he should obiter fall in my Way.

'In answer to yours, if you cannot answer . . . yourself, I will assure you once for all I highly approve and thank you, as I am convinced I always shall when y° act for me, I desire therefore you will always exert unlimited Power on these Occasions.

'With regard to the principal Point, my Health, which I have not yet mentioned, I was tapped again (being the 5th time) at Torbay . . . and possibly here I left the Dropsy, for I have heard nothing of it since. . . .

In Short as we advanced to the South, it is' incredible how my Health advanced with it, and I have no Doubt but that I should have perfectly recovered my Health at this Day, had it not been obstructed by every possible Accident which Fortune could throw in my Way.'

Here a part is missing; and we may take leave to summarize. The first 'accident' was that his whole family, 'except myself [!], Harriot and

Bell' (the maid, Isabella), fell ill. William, the footman, a poor creature, having increased his disorder by indulging too freely in the cheap wines of the country, was seized with a panic apprehension of dying in a foreign land, and becoming an object of unmeasured contempt to his deserted master, took ship in the 'Queen of Portugal' for London. The letter proceeds:

'In the next Place I found myself in the dearest City in the World and in the dearest House in that City. I could not for my Soul live for less than 2 Moidores a day [£2 14*s.*—the old moidore being about 27*s.*] and saw myself likely to be left Pennyless 1,000 miles from home, where I had neither Acquaintance nor Credit among a Set of People who are tearing one another's Souls out for money and ready to deposite Millions with Security but not a Farthing without. In this Condition moreover I saw no Likelihood nor Possibility of changing my Position. The House I was in being the cheapest of the three in which alone I could get a Lodging with^{t} being poisoned.

'Fortune now seemed to take Pity on me, and brought me by a strange Accident acquainted with one Mr. Stubbs,[1] the greatest Merchant of

[1] V. *supra*, p. 140.

this Place, and the greatest Corn factor in the World. He hath a little Kintor [*quinta*[1]] or Villa at a Place called Jonkera [Junqueira], 2 miles from Lisbon and near Bellisle [Belem][2] which is the Kensington of England [Portugal?], and where the Court now reside. Here he likewise got me a little House with^{t} any manner of Furniture not even a Shelf or even a Kitchin Grate. For this I am to pay 9 Moidores a year, and hither I boldly came with scarce suff^{t} Money to buy me the Necessar[ies] of Life. . . .'

At this point we may again abridge. In furnishing the 'villakin,' Fielding's funds sank to the lowest ebb. But a well-timed bill arriving from his brother, the tables were turned, and his expenses became moderate. Instead of two moidores a day, he found he could live for less than a moidore per week, and with difficulty exceed it. 'Where then,' he asks, 'was the Misfortune of all this? or what was there which could retard

[1] A *quinta*, in Spanish and Portuguese, is a small farm or country-house, so called because the tenant pays to the landlord a fifth part of the produce.

[2] Fielding makes the same odd slip in the 'Journal,' adding another by saying that Catherine of Arragon is buried there, whereas he should have written Catherine of Braganza, widow of Charles II. Junqueira is a suburb of Lisbon.

my Recovery, or shock a Philosophy so established as mine which had triumphed over the Terrors of Death when I thought it both certain and near.' The answer is—that Mrs. Fielding, who, as we know, had fallen ill on landing, was still ailing in spirit. The climate of Portugal did not suit her: she was home-sick; and probably yearning for her little family at Fordhook. 'She is,' says Fielding, 'I thank God recovered; but so dispirited that she cries and sighs all Day to return to England,' where she believed her husband might complete his convalescence just as well as at Lisbon, since he could not there readily command a coach, or see after his children and his home. This, to Fielding, who felt himself daily growing stronger, was most disquieting; and far more wearing than it would have been to a more selfish or less warm-hearted man. Matters, moreover, were further complicated by the proceedings of that ambiguous 'another' (the word is Fielding's own), who, either as companion or confidante, plays so disturbing a part in many domestic difficulties. She is not named; but she must, we fear, be identified with Margaret Collier. She was poor; she was pushing and clever; she had become a 'Toast of Lisbon'; and she was apparently steadily setting her cap at the English Resident, one Williamson, a friend of Andrew Millar. Probably knowing that if Fielding went home with his wife and daughter she also would have to accompany them, she seems to have originated the insidious suggestion that Mrs. Fielding should go back alone; and that she (Miss Collier) should remain behind in charge, as companion to Harriot. One can easily imagine the intense vexation that, as hope revived and the pressure of necessity decreased, these unpalatable propositions must have caused to Fielding. 'By these means,' he says, 'my Spirits which were at the Top of the House are thrown down into the Cellar.'[1]

The passages immediately succeeding deal with plans for defeating Miss Collier's machinations. They show much excusable irritation—and even some incoherency. It is obvious, however, that Fielding has not the slightest intention of prejudicing his last chances of recovery by returning prematurely to England. One of the things he wishes his brother to do, is to send him out a 'conversible Man to be my companion in an Evening, with as much of the Qualifications of Learning, Sense, and Good humour as y° can

[1] This must have been a common eighteenth-century figure, for Cradock uses it to describe Sterne.

find, who will drink a moderate Glass in an Evening or will at least sit with me till one when I do.' He does not know, he goes on, anybody more likely to grow better than himself; he has now vigour and elasticity in his limbs;[1] gets easily in and out of a carriage; when in it, can ride the whole day; but all this will be lost if he goes back, or if the schemes of 'another' are allowed to prevail. The letter closes with dispersed particulars of presents, chiefly eatables, which he has despatched to friends in England. The list includes Dr. Collier—'whose very name [he adds] I hate'; and who *may* have been Miss Collier's brother, as her father had long been dead. Then come directions for clothes he desires to have sent out to him, 'for the Winters here are short but cold.' The tailor is to make them wider in the shoulders—a proof that he is putting on flesh. But he must speak for himself:

'Let me have likewise my Tye and a new Mazer Perriwig from Southampton Street, and a new Hat large in the Brim from my Hatter, the corner of Arundel St. I have had a Visit from a Portugese Nobleman, and shall be visited by all as soon as my Kintor is in order. Bell follows

[1] In taking ship at Rotherhithe, he had 'no use of his limbs,' and was hoisted like a log over the side.

Capt Veale to England where he hath promised to marry her. My Family now consists of a black Slave and his Wife, to which I desire you to add a very good perfect Cook, by the first ship, but not by Veale. Scrape together all the Money of mine you can and do not pay a Farthing without my Orders. My Affairs will soon be in a fine Posture, for I can live here, and even make a Figure for almost nothing. In Truth the Produce of the Country is preposterously cheap. I bought three Days ago a Leafe of Partridges [leash—that is, three] for ab^{t} 1.4 English and this Day 5 young Fowls for half a Crown. What is imported from abroad is extravagantly dear, especially what comes from England as doth almost all the provision [?] of Lisbon. I must have from Fordhook likewise 4 Hams a very fine Hog fatted as soon as may be and being cut into Flitches sent me likewise a young Hog made into Pork and salted and pickled in a Tub. A vast large Cheshire cheese and one of Stilton if to be had good and mild. I thank Welch for his, but he was cheated: God bless you and y^{rs} H. Fielding mil annos &c.'

A postscript, of which the end is wanting, reveals further iniquity on the part of William, the footman, who, after his inglorious departure, is found to have cheated his master of £3 12*s.* by pretending that he had discharged an unpaid bill. This sum is to be deducted from any draft he may present for payment; and as a mild punishment, he is to be stripped of his livery. As for Isabella, she is 'only a Fool'; and Fielding wishes her to be provided for at that Universal-Registry-Office in which he and his half-brother were jointly concerned.

Of all these matters there is nothing in the 'Journal,' which ends abruptly with the arrival of the 'Queen of Portugal' at Lisbon. What more came to pass in those brief weeks that followed the despatch of the foregoing letter, will now probably never be revealed. At this date, Fielding, it is clear, firmly believed he should recover. But early in October 1754 his joys and sorrows, his frank delight of living and his unconquerable hopefulness, found their earthly close in the quiet English Cemetery. His widow survived him many years, dying at Canterbury as late as March 1802. Harriot, his daughter, eventually married Colonel James Gabriel Montresor, and lived a brief wedded life. As for Miss Margaret Collier, she retired to Ryde; but scarcely, one would imagine, to meditate the memories of her Peninsular manœuvres. In 1755 she wrote to Richardson, complaining that she had been reported to be the author of the 'Journal,' because 'it was so very bad a performance'—a verdict which the excellent Samuel no doubt heartily approved. Another tradition concerning her is, that a profile she cut in paper supplied the initial hint for Hogarth's posthumous portrait of the author of 'Tom Jones.' As if the marvellous eye-memory of Hogarth could possibly have needed such a stimulus! Whether Captain Richard Veal ever married Isabella Ash, the maid, is not recorded; but from what we know of the antecedents of that septuagenarian lady-killer and ex-privateer, he probably did not. It is, however, to be hoped that the feeble and fraudulent William was duly mulcted in the full amount of which he had sought to 'bubble' his confiding employer.[1]

[1] The two letters referred to in this paper were sold at Sotheby's on Friday, 15th March, 1912, for £305, being Lots 360 and 361 ('Athenaeum,' 23rd March).

THE BAILLI DE SUFFREN

'Pourquoi n'en ai-je pas trouvé un de sa trempe? j'en aurais fait notre Nelson, et les affaires eussent pris un autre tournure!'—NAPOLEON TO LAS CASES AT ST. HELENA.

MONSIEUR PHILIP JAMES DE LOUTHERBOURG, Painter to the King of France, and R.A. of London and Paris, although a naturalized British subject, has been roundly taken to task for depicting, on a canvas at Greenwich Hospital, that 'glorious victory' of the 1st of June 1794, when Richard, Earl Howe, beat the French off Ushant. 'It is disgraceful,' says one of Loutherbourg's French critics, 'for a Frenchman to have made such a picture, when his compatriots, who manned the "Vengeur" at that battle, went down singing the "Marseillaise" rather than lower their colours.'[1] Such, no doubt, was Barrère's boastful report to the National Convention; but modern English historians will hardly accept his version, seeing that the colours *were* lowered and that some three hundred and thirty of the 'Vengeur's' crew were

[1] Dussieux, 'Les Artistes Français à l'Étranger,' 3rd ed. 1876, p. 285.

THE BAILLI DE SUFFREN

(FROM THE PORTRAIT BY GÉRARD)

rescued by the English boats. The remainder did however sink crying 'Vive la République!' like the gallant Frenchmen that they were. And as for Loutherbourg, even if he had not been for twenty years an Englishman by adoption, he was surely justified in painting what he pleased. At any rate, we propose for the moment to take a leaf from his book. It is not to the exploits of Hawke or Boscawen, or Rodney or Duncan or Jervis, that we shall now turn our attention, but to those of a famous French pre-revolutionary sailor, the Bailli de Suffren, who, about 1782-1783, gave us so much trouble in the Bay of Bengal. Valour, decision, energy, initiative—these things have no nationality; and the old Provençal 'sea-hero,' as Carlyle calls him, possessed, in full measure, the great qualities of a great naval commander.

In the opinion of M. Charles Cunat of St. Malo,[1] Suffren's first biographer, himself a retired naval officer, the Bailli's doings by sea and land wholly overshadow those minor details of his career which appeal to 'puerile curiosity' alone.

[1] 'Histoire du Bailli de Suffren," Rennes, 1852. 'Bailli,' it should be explained, is a superior grade in the Knights of St. John of Jerusalem, or Knights of Malta, to which Order Suffren belonged.

'My book,' M. Cunat writes, 'will not contain any of those private facts for which the idle reader seeks in the lives of great men.' Owing to this reserve—which is wise or otherwise according as the reader elects to class himself—the account of the Bailli's early years occupies but a small place in his chronicler's pages. Pierre-André de Suffren Saint-Torpez (later corrupted into Tropez) was the third son of Paul de Suffren, Marquis de Saint-Torpez; and was born on 17th July 1729, at the Château of Saint-Cannat, near Lambesc, in the present department of the Bouches-du-Rhône. Destined from his birth to the sea and the Order of St. John of Jerusalem, he was educated to this end; and at the age of fourteen was sent to Toulon. Entering the navy as a 'garde de la marine' or cadet, he received orders to join the 'Solide,' 64 guns, one of a squadron which the Cabinet of Versailles was equipping to aid the Spanish vessels shut up in Toulon by the Mediterranean fleet under Admiral Mathews. In the indecisive action, or battle of Hyères (February 1744), which followed, ending with the retreat of Mathews, young Suffren received his 'baptism of fire,' the 'Solide' engaging the 'Northumberland;' and, according to M. Cunat, he already displayed the bravery for which he was afterwards so renowned. From the 'Solide' he passed to the 'Pauline,' part of a fleet under Captain Macnamara bound for America. Here again he had fresh experiences of naval warfare. The 'Pauline' laid up, he was transferred to the 'Trident,' 64 guns, Captain d'Estourmel, which, in 1746, set out from Brest with a fleet of thirteen sail, destined to re-capture Cape Breton and break up the English colony of Annapolis. But the expedition was a hopeless failure. The Count de Maurepas, then in charge of the Department of the Marine, had placed at its head the Duc d'Anville, a possibly competent land-officer but a manifestly fresh-water sailor, whose inexperience was not aided by the disloyal officers who resented his command, and even wilfully betrayed him into error. Scurvy, too, broke out in the crews; a storm dispersed the ships, many of which fell into the hands of the enemy; and the discredited remnant returned to Brest. This deplorable disclosure or incapacity, insubordination and general mismanagement made a profound impression on the already observant 'garde de la marine' of the 'Trident,' whose ship was one of those that escaped. But d'Estourmel reported so well of him that he was promoted to a sub-lieutenancy, and in 1747 joined the 'Monarque' (74 guns).

In October of the same year, the 'Monarque' with eight other ships set out from Aix island, at the mouth of the Charente, in charge of 252 sail bound for America. The commander of the little fleet was M. de l'Etanduère, a brave and experienced officer. Off Belle-Isle they were encountered by a British fleet under Admiral Hawke (who had fought as a captain in the battle of Hyères), and on this occasion had Rodney among his subordinates. The English ships greatly outnumbered those of l'Etanduère, who nevertheless contrived to secure the safety of the convoy. On the other hand, six of his ships were captured, one of them being the 'Monarque,' which, beset by three of the enemy at once, and with a dead or dying captain, had been forced to surrender. L'Etanduère's ship, the 'Tonnant,' with the 'Intrépide' (Captain de Vaudreuil), by which he had been most ably seconded, succeeded in getting safely to Brest. Sub-lieutenant de Suffren, who, in after days, never tired of talking of the exploits of the 'Tonnant' and the 'Intrépide,' was carried as a prisoner to England, where he remained until the Peace of Aix-la-Chapelle. He found us 'arrogant,' a not unusual complaint against conquerors; and, it is deplorable to think, henceforth grew to hate us cordially.

There was little reason for love, since the Belle-Isle battle, coupled with Anson's victory off Cape Finisterre in the preceding May over a French fleet carrying supplies to the East Indies, had practically effaced the French fighting navy for a season. And Anson's victory, it is held, had much to do with the establishment of British supremacy in India.

Released in 1748 at the Peace, Suffren, as he had always intended, entered the Order of St. John of Jerusalem; and, being at once admitted as a Knight, was for the next six years occupied in 'caravanning' or convoying trading ships, and fighting the unspeakable Turk. In 1754 he quitted Malta to return to Toulon; and shortly afterwards joined the 'Dauphin Royal.' Sailing in the following year with a squadron for Canada he narrowly escaped being once more taken by the English. The Seven Years' War was brewing though not begun; and Hawke and Boscawen were already engaged in those acts of naval warfare which—according to the point of view—are regarded either as piracy or reprisals. After this, Suffren, now a full lieutenant, was at his own request appointed to the 'Orphée,' one of twelve ships which, with Marshal Richelieu and several thousand men in transports, left Toulon in

April 1756, under Admiral de la Galissonière, in order to invest Minorca—an enterprise successfully accomplished. On 18th May, England definitely declared war; and two days later took place that calamitous engagement in which Byng, with a fleet of thirteen ships and four thousand men, failed both to relieve the garrison of the already-breached fortress of St. Philip at Port Mahon and to defeat la Galissonière. Minorca passed to the French; and Byng retired to Gibraltar. Into the justice or injustice of his subsequent fate on the quarter-deck of the 'Monarque,' it is needless to enter here. A court-martial had acquitted him of cowardice or disaffection, but he could scarcely be cleared from lack of enterprise. La Galisonnière did not long enjoy his first and last triumph, for on his way to the Court at Fontainebleau with the news of his success he died.

Happily for us, however, this French victory was not followed by others. Of Suffren's part in it no record survives, though Byng's deplorable fiasco must assuredly have attracted the attention of an observer whose own defects, as he proved later, were certainly not those of supineness or imperfect energy. He was to have further illustration of these failings in his new commander,

Admiral de la Clue, to whose flagship, the 'Océan,' he passed from the 'Orphée.' M. de la Clue allowed himself to be shut up by Admiral Osborne in Cartagena, from which coign of vantage he, to the intense disgust of Suffren, passively witnessed the capture by the enemy of two of the fleet sent to his assistance. This was in February 1758. A year later the French King's new minister, Choiseul, was equipping his flotilla of flat-bottomed boats to invade England; and England, on her side, was preparing to receive and defeat it. In order to escort it to our shores it was necessary that the Brest and Toulon squadrons should effect a junction. To prevent this, Hawke blockaded Brest; and Boscawen, Toulon; while Rodney busied himself in bombarding Havre de Grâce, where the bulk of the flat-bottoms were congregated together. In August, while Boscawen was refitting at Gibraltar, de la Clue escaped from Toulon, to be chased almost immediately. Either by disaffection or misadventure five of his vessels sought refuge in Cadiz. His rear ship, the 'Centaure,' Captain de Sabran-Grammont, made a most gallant resistance; but two more of the fleet stole away at nightfall. With the four remaining vessels the French admiral ran ashore between Lagos and Cape St. Vincent, where, notwithstanding the neutrality of Portugal, Boscawen burned two and captured the others. One of those burned was the 'Océan'; and Suffren once more saw the inside of an English prison. The projected invasion was of course at an end. More fortunate than Byng, those of the French captains who behaved badly had no worse punishment than the hisses of the mob when they returned to Toulon. Things are not always ordered better in France—though not many years later 'Mr. Yorick' was to say so.

On this second occasion Suffren's confinement in England was brief, and in due time he was released. After some years of inactivity we next find him protecting the commerce of the Mediterranean as commander of a xebec. Then, in 1767, he was promoted to the rank of 'capitaine de frégate.' Slowly gaining the confidence of his superiors, after four more years of fighting the Barbary sea-rovers, a service which earned him the rank of Commander of his Order, he became, in 1772, a 'capitaine de vaisseau,' and in this capacity took part in the evolutions by which the Cabinet of Versailles, still smarting under the humiliations of the Peace of Paris, sought to fortify and train its navy for the further developments of war. In 1776 he commanded the

'Alcméne;' in 1777, the 'Fantasque,' 64 guns. When, in the following year, hostilities again broke out, the 'Fantasque' had joined the squadron of twelve ships of the line and five frigates, which, under the command of Admiral the Count d'Estaing, sailed in April from Toulon to aid the Americans in their struggle for independence. D'Estaing's progress was slow and cautious, and twelve weeks had passed before he reached the Delaware, from which the more expeditious Howe, duly advised of his approach, had retired ten days earlier. In August, Suffren, with the 'Fantasque' and three frigates, was employed to clear Newport Harbour of the little English flotilla stationed there; and the captains burned or sank their vessels to save them from capture by the enemy. During d'Estaing's subsequent operations in the West Indies the 'Fantasque' led the line in the engagement with Admiral Byron before Grenada, receiving the fire of the 'Boyne' and the 'Royal Oak' and losing sixty-two men in killed and wounded. Suffren was afterwards employed by d'Estaing in securing the capitulation of some of the lesser Antilles. With the collapse of d'Estaing's expedition to Georgia, in which Suffren earned further laurels, the French fleet returned home; and in March 1780 Louis XVI, on the report of the French admiral, gave Suffren a pension of 1,500 livres, special stress being laid on his gallantry at Grenada.

His rise had been slow and his recognition tardy, for by this time he was a man of fifty. But, as the old motto in the Tower has it, 'Tout vient à point à qui peult attendre'; and whether he had waited for his opportunity or not, it had come at length. Louis XVI, who took more interest in naval affairs than his contemptible grandfather, had recognized Suffren's worth; and d'Estaing, a brave man if a bad sailor (he had been an officer of cavalry), magnanimously admitted the ability of a frank subordinate who had bluntly criticised the shortcomings of his chief. We may pass briefly over Suffren's next success, the capture of an English convoy off Cape St. Vincent, to pause at what really constitutes the beginning of the most brilliant part of his career. With five ships of the line, a corvette, and a few transports, he was ordered early in 1781 to proceed to the Cape, then a colony of the Dutch, with whom England had just declared war. The French government had learned indirectly that an expedition, under the well-known Commodore or 'Governor' George Johnstone, was fitting out to seize this coveted halting-place on the road to India; and Suffren's mission was to secure its safety. On March 22 he sailed from Brest with the Count de Grasse's fleet, which was bound for the West Indies. Off the Azores they parted company, de Grasse going westward, Suffren to the south. One of his ships, the 'Artésien,' was found to be short of water; and Suffren, now 'chef d'escadre' or commodore, decided to put in at the Portuguese colony of Porto Praya in the Cape Verd Islands. Here Johnstone, making for the Cape, had arrived a few days earlier, with five ships, several frigates and a number of armed transports. Relying too implicitly on the supposed secrecy of his enterprise and the neutrality of the port, he lay quietly at anchor, wholly unprepared for attack. Both commanders were naturally taken by surprise. But Suffren was neither a d'Anville nor a de la Clue, and his decision was promptly arrived at. Porto Praya, it is true, was in neutral water. But the lieutenant of the 'Océan' remembered Boscawen and Lagos Bay. Signalling promptly to his captains to follow, he steered straight into the harbour; anchored as close as he could to the English flagship; and, regardless of the guns of the English squadron, the armed transports, and the Portuguese fortress, opened a vigorous fire. Unhappily he was not seconded with equal alacrity. The

M

'Annibal,' which came close after him and whose captain was soon killed, by some misconception lost time; the 'Vengeur' and the 'Sphinx,' the two rear ships, scarcely got into action at all; while the 'Artésien,' mistaking in the smoke an East Indiaman for a man-of-war, drifted out of the combat altogether. At the end of an hour's fighting, Suffren, having battered the enemy to his heart's content, and finding himself with only two ships, one of which, the 'Annibal,' had lost her main- and mizen-masts, judged it expedient to cut his cables and make off. This he did, as swiftly as he came, followed by the 'Annibal,' which, in escaping, lost her remaining mast, but was fortunately taken in tow by the unoccupied 'Sphinx.' The 'Héros' herself had been roughly handled. But Suffren had accomplished more than he knew. For though Johnstone, recovering himself, started in pursuit, he was prudent enough to abandon his designs on the Cape; and Suffren's bold resolve to fight then and there was amply justified by the event. Had he been effectually supported by his subordinates, he would probably have succeeded in wholly destroying Johnstone's squadron.

On 21st June 1781 he reached Simon's Bay, and having satisfied himself of the immunity of the Cape from further attack, sailed for the

Mauritius, arriving in October. Here the Count d'Orves, a man broken in health and of declining energy but a senior in rank, took over the command of the combined fleet, which consisted of eleven ships of the line, three frigates, three corvettes and a fire-ship. When Suffren's needful repairs were completed, it set sail for India to help the famous Sultan of Mysore, Haidar Ali, in his efforts to drive the English out of the Carnatic. On the way (22nd January 1782) Suffren chased and captured an English fifty-gun ship, the 'Hannibal,' the command of which eventually fell to the de Galles, who after the captain's death had so gallantly fought the French 'Annibal' at Porto Praya. This prize added another battleship to the side of the French. On 9th February d'Orves died, and his death placed Suffren in supreme command. A few days later Suffren sighted Madras, where he hoped to surprise the English fleet before it could shelter itself under the formidable batteries of Black Town and Fort St. George. But as things fell out, by this time the English fleet, numbering nine large ships of war, was already occupying the desired position; and was lying, not dispersedly, as at Porto Praya, but in order of battle.

The leader, too, was of tougher temper than Johnstone, and a foe in many respects worthy of

Suffren's steel. Sir Edward Hughes, Knight of the Bath, and Vice-Admiral of the Blue, had been Commander-in-Chief in the East Indies since 1778, and at sea had hitherto had matters very much his own way. Two years earlier he had destroyed Haidar's fleet at Mangalore. Subsequently, on hearing of the outbreak of war between England and Holland, he had helped Sir Hector Munro to reduce the Dutch settlement of Negapatam on the Coromandel coast. He had then proceeded to Trincomali in Ceylon, which he reached in January 1782, at once occupying the town. The Dutch, however, withdrew to Fort Osnaburg, which Hughes stormed successfully a few days later. Returning after this exploit to Madras, he reached it a few days before the already recorded arrival of Suffren. His fleet had been reinforced by three more ships from England, and when he anchored under the guns of the Madras forts he had been forewarned of the advent of the French. And thus began the series of remarkable naval engagements which, inconclusive though they proved, reflected honour on both sides, and which only came to an end with the Peace of Versailles. Both commanders were men of exceptional ability. Hughes was a skilled seaman with a great deal of cautious tenacity; and Suffren, with all the ardour and verve of his nation, was 'brave as his sword.' His tactics and strategy are admitted to have been far superior to those of his opponent; but Hughes had an advantage in the better discipline and steadiness of his subordinates.

Rightly regarding the English admiral's position as unassailable, Suffren, after a council of war, weighed anchor, and went south to Trincomali, guessing, no doubt, that Hughes would follow, which he did. Slipping past the French fleet in the night, he found at daybreak on 17th February that, by the carelessness of one of the French captains, the convoy had become separated from the fleet. Chasing it forthwith, he took six ships, five of which were English prizes. The sixth, the French transport 'Lauriston,' was more valuable still, since, besides a train of artillery and military stores, destined for Haidar Ali, she had on board three hundred soldiers of the Lausanne regiment. As Hughes expected, Suffren came swiftly to the rescue; and a struggle ensued between the French van of seven ships and the English rear and centre of five, the four foremost of the English line never being able to tack and come into action. Suffren himself in the 'Héros' engaged Hughes's flagship the 'Superb,' but the brunt of battle was borne by the 'Exeter,' the sternmost English ship, which was assailed successively by several of the enemy, the 'Orient' and the 'Petit Annibal' (the 'Hannibal' prize) distinguishing themselves particularly. Much damage was done on both sides, though the English suffered most. The 'Superb' lost her captain and two lieutenants, and owing to shot-holes in the hull had five feet of water in the hold; while the unfortunate 'Exeter' was pounded to a hulk. Hughes' tactics, if not ill-judged, at least proved unfortunate; his rear was terribly overmatched; but the ships were fought splendidly, and it was not overwhelmed. Suffren had again to complain of the inadequate support he received from his captains. Five of his twelve ships remained inactive 'spectateurs du combat,' disregarding the signals to come to close quarters, and firing ineffectively from a distance. Towards six in the evening, therefore, when a change of wind made it probable that the English vanguard could intervene, Suffren ceased fighting. The total loss on the French side amounted to thirty killed and a hundred wounded; and it is naturally contended by Suffren's French biographer that Suffren, even without the support of his rearguard, could have destroyed or hopelessly crippled the English fleet. There must however have been other considerations which induced him to close the action.[1]

This was the first of what Carlyle calls his 'six *non-defeats*'—for Carlyle includes Porto Praya with the five actions which subsequently took place with Hughes. After that just described, which is spoken of indifferently as off Sadras or Fort St. George, Hughes went to refit in the sheltered harbour of Trincomali, and Suffren sailed to Pondicherry to effect negotiations with Haidar Ali. His desire was that the land forces from France should re-capture that Negapatam which not many months before the English admiral had helped to wrest from the Dutch. But M. Duchemin, who commanded the troops, preferred to attack the nearer Cuddalore or Goudelour. With the consent of the Sultan this course was

[1] We may here recall—since M. Cunat is generous enough to do so—an English incident of this engagement off Sadras, as related in Beatson ('Naval and Military Memoirs of Great Britain,' 1804, p. 576). When Commodore King of the 'Exeter,' whose second-in-command, Captain Reynolds, had been killed at his side by a cannon-shot, was asked by the Master what could possibly be done with a ship little better than a floating wreck, he answered calmly: 'There is nothing to be done but fight her till she sink!' It is pleasant to think that George III made King, Sir Richard; and that he survived till 1806.

accordingly taken. The soldiers were landed at Porto Novo, taking Cuddalore on 4th April. These transactions had necessarily occupied some time; and in the interim Hughes, rapidly recouping at Trincomali, had returned to Madras, where his fleet was augmented from England by the 'Magnanime' and the 'Sultan.' He then again started for Trincomali with troops and stores. On the 8th he sighted the French fleet, of whom he had hitherto heard nothing, and on the 12th a second action took place near the island of Providien, off Ceylon. 'This,' says Admiral Mahan, 'was the hardest fight between these two hard fighters'; and it happened on the very day that Rodney defeated and captured de Grasse off Dominica. The French had twelve ships, the English eleven. After some preliminary manœuvring, the battle began a little after noon. Hughes's line was formed in good order, at two cables' length distance, the 'Superb' (74) occupying the centre of the line, with the 'Monmouth' (64) ahead and 'Monarca' (74) astern. Five of the French engaged the English van; while the remaining seven, led by Suffren himself, bore down on the three ships mentioned above. The 'Héros,' and its second, the 'Orient,' attacked the 'Superb' within pistol shot, and for nine minutes a furious fire was exchanged. Then Suffren, leaving his rear to continue the conflict with the 'Superb' and the 'Monarca,' devoted his energies to the lesser 'Monmouth,' whose captain, James Alms, had fought under Johnstone at Porto Praya, and, under Hughes, had captured the six prizes at Fort St. George. Already assailed by one of the French fleet, the 'Monmouth' was speedily reduced to a wreck. With her wheel shot away and her masts gone, her flag nailed to one stump and a rag of sail hoisted on another, she lay like a log on the water, until a lucky gust of wind enabled Captain Hawker of the English 'Hero' to tow her into a position of comparative security. Out of an effective crew of 400 she had 147 killed and wounded; in fact, the bulk of the casualties were divided between the 'Monmouth' and the flagship. The French 'Héros' must also have fared badly, for Suffren had to transfer his flag to another ship. Later in the day the fleets fell apart, and the battle was not renewed. Each side claimed the advantage; but, once again, either from disaffection, or that excessive caution which Suffren stigmatized as 'the veil of timidity,' he was ill served by his captains.

The next two actions between Suffren and Hughes may be more briefly dealt with. The first, on 6th July, took place off Negapatam, which was still a cherished French objective. Hughes, contrary to his custom, began the attack on this occasion; and the fleets engaged line to line, only to be thrown into hopeless disorder, after an obstinate two hours' struggle, by a sudden change of wind in which they drew off, as before, with contradictory results. Suffren regarded himself as master of the field: Hughes reported to the Admiralty that he had obtained a decisive superiority. But in either case the French operations against Negapatam were for the time abandoned. In this fight occurred the equivocal incident of the 'Sévère' (64), which, finding herself opposed to the 'Sultan' (74) and other English ships, hauled down her colours by order of her commander, M. de Cillart. They were immediately rehoisted by his indignant subordinates, and the 'Sévère' recommenced firing. An interchange of recrimination ensued between the admirals on the subject; but M. de Cillart was suspended and eventually dismissed the service. He was not the sole offender, for no fewer than four French captains were broke by Suffren and sent to the Mauritius.[1]

[1] In the Painted Hall at Greenwich Hospital there is a picture of the action off Negapatam by Dominic Serres, R.A.

Hughes retired to Madras to refit, and the French went to Cuddalore. Having been baulked in the attempt on Negapatam, Suffren turned his attention to Trincomali; and in this instance contrived to anticipate Hughes. Reinforced at Batticaloa from France on 21st August,[1] he sailed for Trincomali, before which he arrived on the 25th. Vigorously attacked, the place speedily surrendered; and when, on 3rd September, Hughes made his appearance, the French flag was floating from Fort Osnaburg. The fight that followed was again indecisive. The fleets were fifteen French to twelve English. Suffren's tactics, as at Sadras and Providien, were to assail the enemy's rear. But excellent as they had proved, they were fruitless in face of the jealousy or ill-will of some of his captains, whose discontent by this time had grown to a cabal. After a precipitate and disorderly combat, the French fighting falling almost wholly on the flagship 'Heros,' the 'Illustre' and the 'Ajax,' the wind changed, and the fleets separ-

As Serres had been a seaman, and as the picture was the bequest of Admiral Hughes, it may be presumed to be accurate. Hughes, who survived until 1794, also left his portrait by Reynolds to the Hospital.

[1] On the 19th of this month he had received, from the Grand Master of the Order of St. John of Jerusalem, his commission as Bailli, the next grade to that of the head.

ated, the French going back to Trincomali and the English to Madras. Suffren's disappointment knew no bounds, and his words have all the emphasis of his anger:

'My heart [he wrote] is wrung by the most general defection. I have just lost the opportunity of destroying the English squadron. . . All—yes, all—might have got near, since we were to windward and ahead, and none did so. Several among them had behaved bravely in other combats. I can only attribute this horror to the wish to bring the cruise to an end, to ill-will and to ignorance; for I dare not suspect anything worse. The result has been terrible. I must tell you, Monseigneur, that officers who have been long at the Isle of France are neither seamen nor military men. Not seamen, for they have not been at sea; and the trading temper, independent and insubordinate, is absolutely opposed to the military spirit.[1]

The fight off Trincomali took place in September 1782, and it was nearly nine months before the rivals met again. In returning to Trincomali, Suffren, by the fault of the commander, lost the 'Orient,' one of his best ships; and he afterwards

[1] Quoted in Admiral Mahan's 'Influence of Sea Power upon History,' 6th ed. p. 435.

lost another at Cuddalore. Hughes, having no longer a base in Ceylon, had to go round to Bombay—not without difficulties in the stormy season. Consequently he missed Sir Richard Bickerton, who, arriving from England with reinforcements and stores, and failing to find Hughes in the Bay of Bengal, had to follow him to Bombay.[1] Suffren, on the other hand, wintered in Sumatra, where he was more on the spot than his adversary. In December 1782 Haidar Ali died, and the succession passed to his arrogant son, Tipu Saib. With June 1783 the fortune of war had centred round Cuddalore, where, by land, Coote's successor, Stuart, with a superior force, was beleaguering the Marquis de Bussy; and off Cuddalore on the 20th, Hughes and Suffren met for the last time. The encounter 'was of the commonplace eighteenth century order—save for two details.' One was, that in pursuance of orders from Versailles arising out of the capture of the Count de Grasse at Dominica by Rodney, Suffren directed operations, not from the flagship in the line, but from the 'Cléopatre,' a frigate outside it. The other was that 'the French fleet of fifteen

[1] One of Bickerton's relief fleet was the 'Bristol,' whose captain was Fanny Burney's brother James. In the battle of Cuddalore the 'Bristol' engaged the 'Hardi.'

sail attacked the British fleet of eighteen from windward—and it was the British fleet which retired.'[1] Five days later Hughes wrote to Suffren announcing the conclusion of peace, and suggesting a suspension of hostilities.

Hughes was probably not sorry for the turn things had taken, for the struggle had been difficult and protracted, and some of his crews had suffered terribly from sickness. There are also indications that Suffren himself did not regard the future outlook as hopeful. 'God be praised for the peace!' he wrote, 'for it was clear that in India, though we had the means to impose the law, all would have been lost.' 'War alone,' he added significantly, 'can make bearable the weariness of certain things.' Fighting, however, was now for the time at an end; and in October 1783, he set out for France, stopping at the Mauritius and the Cape. The passage home was a prolonged triumph. Everywhere 'the winds Blew his own praises in his eyes.' Especially was he gratified by the frank cordiality of his old opponents, the English. At Table Bay the captains of nine of Hughes's ships, with Commodore King of the 'Exeter' at their head, called eagerly

[1] Hannay's 'Short History of the Royal Navy,' 1909, ii, 291.

upon him. 'The good Dutchmen have received me as their deliverer,' he wrote; 'but among the tributes which have most flattered me, none has given me more pleasure than the esteem and consideration testified by the English who are here.' At Paris, which he reached in April 1784, the story is the same. When he appeared at Versailles, the 'gardes-du-corps,' hearing his name, rose in a body and, quitting their weapons, escorted him to the audience. Louis XVI received him most warmly; and Marie Antoinette herself presented him to the Dauphin with the words, 'This is M. de Suffren, one of the men who has best served the King.' And when the little boy (it must have been the first Dauphin, then four years old) hesitated in repeating the name: 'My son,' said the Queen, 'you must learn early to hear pronounced, and yourself to pronounce the name of the hero-defenders of their country.' The Countess d'Artois, and her son, the young Duke d'Angoulême, were equally amiable; and there was a universal rain of compliments. At a dinner given by the Minister of Marine, d'Estaing, the Bailli's old commander, being addressed as 'mon général,' replied, with happy adroitness, that M. de Suffren was the only 'general' present. The King created for him a special and personal office of Vice-Admiral of France; and made him a Knight of the Order of the Saint-Esprit. Carmontelle sketched him for the Orléans collection; his portrait was painted by François Gérard, and at Salon, near his Provençal birth-place, his bust by Foucou was placed in the Hôtel de Ville. Lastly, the Estates of his native Provence struck a magnificent medal in his honour, crediting him largely with the protection of the Cape, the taking of Trincomali, the relief of Cuddalore, the defence of India, and six glorious combats. The States-General of Holland also presented him with a medal.[1]

To all these distinctions there came in short space a mournful sequel. The Bailli's duties as Vice-Admiral detained him in Paris, where, for a few years, he lived quietly in the Hôtel Montmorency at the entrance of the rue de la Chaussée d'Antin. With 1788 the war-cloud again began to darken the horizon; and he was deputed by

[1] That ships should be called after him was to be expected; and in 1793 a 'Suffren' of seventy-four guns was launched at Brest. But, in 1794, it was decided that 'the name of a ci-devant noble' could not properly figure among republican designations, and the 'Suffren' became the 'Redoutable.' The 'Redoutable' (Captain Lucas) took part in the battle of Trafalgar, and from her mizen-top came the musket-ball that killed Nelson.

Louis XVI to superintend the equipment of a considerable fleet at Brest. In December, while engaged on these duties, he died unexpectedly, and was buried quietly on the 10th in the Church of Sainte-Marie-du-Temple. The cause of death was declared to be apoplexy—in his case only too probable. No suspicion seems to have been aroused at the time; and it was not until more than forty years afterwards that M. Jal, the historiographer of the French navy, published a different account. According to this, Suffren was killed in a duel by the Prince de Mirepoix, who had invoked his good offices on behalf of two nephews then under sentence for dereliction of duty in India. The Bailli had refused to intervene; and refused in such terms as, in those days, could only provoke a demand for satisfaction. Honour forbade him to decline the challenge, although his age (he was in his sixtieth year), and his excessive corpulence, wholly unfitted him for any encounter of the kind. As a result, he was mortally wounded, and succumbed in a couple of days. This version of his fate is now generally accepted. The solitary witness, it is true, is Dehodencq, an old servant in Suffren's household, who repeated his story for many years without variation. There were no motives on his part for inventing it, while there were several for its suppression; and it was a plausible feature of the narrative that the Bailli himself had, on his deathbed, enjoined those about him to preserve absolute secrecy in the matter.[1]

But whether the Bailli de Suffren died in deference to a deplorable social code, or in the ordinary course of nature, he was a man of whom France has every reason to be proud. In the period of moral disintegration, of incompetence in high places, of inequitable privileges and tyrannous traditions, which heralded the outbreak of the French revolution, it was something to be a single-minded patriot, putting duty before titles of distinction, and love of country before personal advancement. Suffren was this—and more. He may have been brusque and eccentric—he was a blunt seaman, with his heart in his work; he may, as Admiral Mahan thinks, have 'expected too much of his captains'—without training them to do better; but he was a great military genius, having all the indispensable equipment of rapid perception, clear judgment, prompt decision and

[1] Jal, 'Scènes de la Vie Maritime,' 1832, vol. iii, p. 161; Cunat, 345 *et seq.*; and Jal again, 'Dict. Critique,' etc., 2nd ed. 1872, pp. 1155-7. See Appendix C (Death of the Bailli de Suffren).

inflexibility of purpose. The old dilatory methods of maritime warfare were too slow for his fiery and impetuous southern temperament. Restive under inaction—as he had often reason to be—he trusted to attack rather than defence; and though a skilful strategist on occasion, preferred bold and even hazardous measures to formal evolutions, manœuvres, and 'bookish theoric.' Had he been better backed from home—had he been better served afloat, he might, as he hoped, have succeeded in 'destroying the English squadron,' with results to our supremacy in the East which, fortunately, it is now only possible to conjecture.

EIGHTEENTH-CENTURY STOWE

'A Work to wonder at—perhaps a STOWE.'—*Pope.*

IN one of Horace Walpole's letters to George Montagu, dated July 1770, there is a passage which might well serve as a perpetual preface to any account of the once-famous Buckinghamshire mansion known as Stowe. The letter relates how the writer was 'requisitioned' by his beloved 'Princess Amélie,' George II.'s daughter, to accompany a select party on a five days' visit to Lord Temple's country-seat. They walked or drove about the grounds, drank coffee at the triumphal arch which their host had erected in the Princess's honour, fished fitfully in the lake, 'played at pharaoh till ten,' and altogether amused themselves consumedly. 'We laughed a great deal, and had not a cloud the whole time.' Then comes the particular passage indicated above: 'The number of buildings and variety of scenes in the garden made each day different from the rest; and my meditations on so historic a spot prevented my being tired. Every acre brings to one's mind some instance of the . . . greatness or miscarriages of those that have inhabited, decorated, planned, or visited the place. Pope, Congreve, Vanbrugh, Kent, Gibbs, Lord Cobham, Lord Chesterfield, the mob of nephews, the Lytteltons, Grenvilles, Wests, 'Leonidas' Glover and Wilkes, the late Prince of Wales, the King of Denmark, Princess Amélie . . . [all these, says Walpole,] add visionary personages to the charming scenes, that are so enriched with fanes and temples, that the real prospects are little less than visions themselves.' To revive Walpole's reminiscences—reminiscences, it should be added, not always consistent—one must be Walpole. But we may fairly attempt to recall some of the people and things he mentions.

The Temples of Stowe in Bucks and of Cobham in Kent traced their lineage, if not to Inachus, at least to that historic Leofric, Earl of Chester and Mercia, who had to wife the Godgifu or Godiva of legend. For the moment, however, we need go no farther back than the reign of James I, when, after various vicissitudes, the estate of Stowe had passed definitely to the Temples in the person of Thomas Temple of Stowe and Burton Dasset, Knight and Baronet. This Sir Thomas

Temple married Hester, daughter of Miles Sandys of Latimers on the Chess, a lady who, herself having a family of thirteen, and surviving through four generations, was privileged to behold no fewer than seven hundred of her descendants, a fact for the veracity of which Thomas Fuller in his 'Worthies' vouches quaintly by declaring that he bought the knowledge with the loss of a wager. To Sir Thomas succeeded his son, Sir Peter, who enclosed some two hundred acres of ground for a park; while the next heir, Sir Richard Temple the first, rebuilt what had been the Manor House. From him, in 1697, the property passed to Sir Richard Temple the second, later the Lord Cobham of whom Walpole speaks; and with this Sir Richard, a distinguished soldier and statesman, the history of Stowe is connected for more than half a century. Entering the army early, he was present at the sieges of Ruremonde and Venloo; and when, in 1708, Lille was taken by the Allies, his bearing as Brigadier-General justified Marlborough in making him the messenger to Queen Anne of the fall of that fortress. He was created Baron Cobham at the accession of George I, and to announce that fact went as Envoy Extraordinary and Plenipotentiary to Charles VI, Emperor of Germany. In 1718 he became a Viscount. But it is needless to rehearse his further honours, which were many. Among other things, he was Colonel of the 'King's Own,' or Cobham's troop of horse (1st Dragoon Guards), in which his connection, William Pitt, afterwards first Earl of Chatham, but then engrossed in the study of military manuals, rode as a cornet. After becoming Constable of Windsor Castle and Governor of Jersey, Cobham fell into disgrace under George II for his opposition to the Excise Bill. This turned him into the Coryphæus of the little knot of youthful politicians, generally his own relatives, whom Sir Robert Walpole contemptuously called the 'Boy Patriots.' By 1742 he was a Field-Marshal; and during the King's absence in Hanover, was appointed one of the Regents. He died in 1749, and was buried at Stowe. Most of the intervals of his active life had been passed there in entertaining his friends, enlarging the buildings, and elaborating those spacious gardens which, even in an epoch of magnificent rural 'retirements,' rendered the place a permanent centre of attraction.

At the close of the eighteenth century, the ornamental grounds of Stowe (with which, following the old contemporary guide-books, it is convenient to begin, occupied some four hundred acres, and were in part surrounded by a sunk fence, on the inner side of which was a wide, elm-shaded gravel-walk. When Sir Richard Temple first entered on his tenancy, the formal horticultural models favoured by William and Anne were in full vogue; and the place was laid out much after the Dutch fashion adopted by London and Wise at Kensington Palace and elsewhere. But under the first George, Charles Bridgeman, the royal head-gardener, became also the presiding spirit at Stowe. He it was who probably instituted the above-mentioned sunk fence, a device borrowed from the military art; and he went on gradually to blend the landscape with the garden, and to substitute lawns and vistas for pleached alleys and precise flower beds.[1] When, in 1738, Bridgeman died, he was succeeded by Lancelot, afterwards known as 'Capability' Brown, who, beginning modestly, ultimately attained the position of resident gardener-in-chief. Under Brown, the ruralising of the place continued; and the opening of effective points of view, the planting out of unpicturesque

[1] In 1848 his original plans and drawings for Stowe were still in existence. They had been engraved by Rigaud and Baron in 1739.

objects, the creation of hollows and hillocks, cascades and lakes, were carried forward systematically. Lastly, or rather concurrently, were erected those characteristic 'fanes and temples' spoken of by Walpole, rendering the spot, in the words of another chronicler, 'when beheld from a distance . . . like a vast grove, interspersed with columns, obelisks, and towers, which apparently emerge from a luxuriant mass of foliage.'

In promoting these developments it is probable that Bridgeman and Brown were largely advised and aided by another eminent votary of the new methods in gardening, the multifarious William Kent, who is also primarily responsible for most of the dispersed buildings, although it is not always easy to fix the exact date of their construction. But as Vanbrugh, to whom some of them confessedly belong, died in 1726, and Kent himself in 1748, it may safely be concluded that the structures associated with their names are contemporary with Lord Cobham, as he, too, died in 1749. The squat little Temple of Bacchus overlooking the lake, and decorated by the 'alti-rilievi' of that elder Nollekens who died from terror of the '45; the Rotundo, with its dome and delicate Ionic columns; and the two Boycott pavilions,[1] were certainly designed by Vanbrugh, although they appear to have been modified in construction by the Signor Borra (sometime architect to the King of Sardinia), who accompanied 'Palmyra' Wood in his Syrian researches. But the majority of the other Cobham erections emanated from the fertile brain of Kent. Kent it was who planned the entrance Lodges, the artificial Ruins, the Hermitage, the Grotto; the temple of Venus, adorned appropriately with frescoes by Joseph Slater from Spenser's 'Faerie Queene'; the temple of Ancient Virtue, equipped with full-length statues by Peter Scheemakers of Homer, Socrates, Lycurgus, and Epaminondas; and the temple of British Worthies. Other buildings were the temple of Friendship, consecrated to the somewhat variable company of Lord Cobham's friends, and including busts of Pitt, Chesterfield, and Lyttelton;[2] the monument to his nephew, Captain Thomas Grenville, who died fighting the French under Anson in May 1747, and the monument erected in 1736 'moribus ur-

[1] So called from a hamlet which had been absorbed in the Stowe property.

[2] 'The marbles were usually designated by the labourers who showed the gardens as the "Bustesses of my lord's acquaintances"' ('Stowe Catalogue,' 1848, p. xxxii).

banis, candidis, facillimis' of William Congreve. This stood on an island in the upper lake. Surmounted by a monkey inspecting himself in a mirror, and ornamented with dramatic accessaries, it was one of the least happy of Kent's performances, though it perhaps scarcely deserved the condemnation of Macaulay, who calls it, in his best sledge-hammer manner, 'the ugliest and most absurd of the buildings at Stowe.' The Latin quotation reminds us that all the aforesaid edifices were lavishly decorated with similar inscriptions; and that some of those in English were by Sir George, afterwards Lord Lyttelton, who was the son of Lord Cobham's sister, Christian. One of the love-poems addressed by Lyttelton to that charming Lucy Fortescue, whom he afterwards married, and beginning

> Fair Venus, whose delightful Shrine surveys
> Its front reflected in the silver lake,

was a direct invocation of the Stowe divinity.

Lord Cobham seems to have regarded the monument of Congreve as an adequate memorial, for he figured neither in the temple of British Worthies nor the temple of Friendship. But they were close friends nevertheless, although the records of their intercourse are apparently confined to a couple of entries in the 'Journal to Stella.' In 1730 an unknown rhymer composed, and Curll printed, a long and rather dreary 'Epistle to Lord Viscount Cobham, in Memory of his Friend, the late Mr. Congreve,' in which he says:

> Thee early, and thee last his tuneful Breath
> Addrest with grateful Notes—till stopt by Death;

the references being to Congreve's 'Art of Pleasing' and to his imitation of Horace's 'Epistle to Tibullus,' one inscribed to Cobham early in Congreve's career, the other composed not long before his death. Johnson, whose attitude to Congreve, if intelligible, is extremely unsympathetic, flatly condemns the 'Art of Pleasing.' "It is founded,' he says, 'on a vulgar but perhaps impracticable principle, and the staleness of the sense is not concealed by any novelty of illustration or elegance of diction.' But, even though it be no more than an imitation, there is surely aphoristic compactness in the couplet,

> None are, for being what they are, in fault,
> But for not being what they wou'd be thought,—

which has also the subordinate merit of illustrating that old eighteenth-century pronunciation of 'fault' to be found in Pope, Prior, and Goldsmith. Johnson is, besides, mistaken in saying that Congreve, apart from his plays, never penned a memorable couplet. Even as regards the poems, this is not borne out by modern dictionaries of quotations; while the playwright who has endowed the language with 'Music has charms to soothe a savage breast,' and the line as to 'marrying in haste' and 'repenting at leisure,' can afford to rest upon his laurels as a crystallizer of the 'wisdom of many.' The epistle also refers to Cobham's gifts as a critic, gifts to be presently illustrated in his correspondence with Pope. But with the statement that Cobham was a pall-bearer at Congreve's burial in Westminster Abbey, we have exhausted the record of their relations.

The 'Journal to Stella,' however, suggests the name of Swift. Was Swift one of Stowe's habitués? He certainly knew Temple in 1710, for he speaks of meeting him in October of that year at a 'blind tavern,'[1] where he was drinking bad punch with Congreve and Dick Estcourt the player. 'The knight [Temple] sent for six flasks of his own wine for me, and we staid till twelve.'[2] Ten days later he is dining at Temple's house

[1] This seems to mean no more than an obscure house.

[2] The custom of drinking one's own wine at a tavern seems peculiar; but there are several references to it in

with Congreve and Vanbrugh. As regards the latter he says, 'We were very civil and cold,' which is perhaps to be expected. It is hard to be effusively cordial to a critic who has likened one's architectural efforts to a 'goose pie,'[1] as Swift had, a year or two before, in those sarcastic lines on the house in Scotland Yard which Vanbrugh had thrown together for himself out of the ruins of Whitehall Palace. What made matters worse was, that the Duchess of Marlborough, for whom Vanbrugh was already building Blenheim under difficulties, persisted in teasing him on the subject, which, says Swift, had made him angry, 'though he be a good-natured fellow.' There is only one more reference to Temple in the 'Journal,' and after 1727 Swift never returned to England. But of Cobham's intercourse with Pope there are further particulars, though of a later date. In Pope's last

the 'Diary' (Ashton's 'Social Life in the Reign of Queen Anne, 1883, 177). Readers of 'Pendennis' may remember that, according to Mr. Wagg, Lord Steyne was in the habit of sending his own wine to people with whom he was in the habit of dining (ch. xxxv).

[1] At length they in the Rubbish spy
A Thing resembling a Goose Py.
'Vanbrugh's House,' 1706.

letter to Swift he speaks of himself as "generally rambling in the summer for a month to Lord Cobham's, the Bath, or elsewhere,' and in a letter of 1735 to Caryll, we get some hint of the beginning of the friendship. Pope has known Lord Cobham ten years, he says, without writing three letters to him; and he adds that he esteems him as much as any friend he has, and that he is going to stay three weeks with him, namely, at Stowe, which he did, meeting Lady Suffolk.[1] From another letter he had been there in the previous year; and earlier still he tells Martha Blount how he is drawn about by an ancient horse, then used in rolling the gardens, but which had once carried James Radcliffe, third Earl of Derwentwater, when he was made prisoner at Preston.[2] In 1739 another letter informs her that he is staying at Stowe 'en petit comité' with Lady Cobham, and her relative, that Henrietta Jane Speed whose charms and 'bric-à-brac,'—to say nothing of £30,000—seem, a few years afterwards, to have had a transitory attraction for Gray. 'All the mornings we breakfast and dis-

[1] 'Suffolk Correspondence,' 1824, ii, 143.

[2] Probably an old trooper's-horse, for Cobham's dragoons seem to have been at Preston ('Diary of Lady Cowper,' 1864, 188).

pute; after dinner, and at night, music and harmony; in the garden, fishing; no politics and no cards, nor much reading. This agrees exactly with me; for the want of cards sends us early to bed.' As to the garden, it 'is beyond all description.' He is in it every hour but dinner and night, and every hour envying himself the delight because not partaken by his correspondent, who would *see* it better. 'Adieu,' he says at the close 'I am going to the Elysian Fields [a part of the grounds], where I shall meet your idea'—by which, no doubt, he means her Platonic archetype.

In the Epistle to Lord Burlington that satirizes the vacuous magnificence of 'Timon's villa' at Edgware, Pope, by contrast, sketches at once the rival beauties of Stowe, and lays down the laws of landscape gardening:

> To build, to plant, whatever you intend,
> To rear the Column, or the Arch to bend,
> To swell the Terrace, or to sink the Grot;
> In all, let Nature never be forgot.
> But treat the Goddess like a modest fair,
> Nor over-dress, nor leave her wholly bare;
> Let not each Beauty ev'rywhere be spy'd,
> Where half the Skill is decently to hide.
> He gains all Points, who pleasingly confounds,
> Surprises, varies and conceals the Bounds.

Consult the Genius of the Place in all;
That tells the Waters or to rise, or fall;
Or helps th' ambitious Hill the heav'ns to scale,
Or scoops in circling theatres the Vale;
Calls in the Country, catches op'ning glades,
Joins willing Woods, and varies shades from shades;
Now breaks, or now directs, th' intending Lines;
Paints as you plant, and, as you work, designs.
Still follow Sense, of ev'ry Art the Soul,
Parts answ'ring parts shall slide into a whole,
Spontaneous beauties all around advance,
Start ev'n from Difficulty, strike from Chance;
Nature shall join you, Time shall make it grow
A Work to wonder at—perhaps a STOWE.

Two years later, in 1733, Pope inscribed to Cobham a special Epistle, 'On the Knowledge and Characters of Men,' afterwards printed as the first of the Moral Essays; and to this relate the only two letters from Lord Cobham to the poet which have been preserved. In both, Cobham shows the critical faculty with which Congreve had credited him; and Pope seems to have acted on his suggestions. 'As I remember, when I saw the "Brouillon" of this epistle,' writes Cobham, 'it was perplexed; you have now made it the contrary, and I think it is the clearest and the cleanest[1]

[1] This is an odd word, and one almost fancies that Ruffhead ('Life of Pope,' 1769, 275), who first printed these letters, mis-copied. 'Cleanest,' in the sense of least

of all you have wrote. From a sentence in the second letter it would almost appear that Pope's famous Oldfield couplets ('Odious! in woollen! 'twould a Saint provoke!')[1] were the result of a hint by Cobham that the poet should introduce 'an old Lady dressing her silver locks with pink, and ordering her coffin to be lined with white quilted sattin with gold fringes.' But the most material lines are those in which, by an adroit transition from censure to compliment, Pope concludes his impeachment of the 'ruling passion':

> And you! brave COBHAM, to the latest breath,
> Shall feel your ruling passion strong in death:
> Such in those moments as in all the past,
> 'Oh, save my Country, Heav'n!' shall be your last.

'Whatever were the precise last words of

objectionable, is unlikely; and in the sense of 'clearest,' would be tautological. Can Cobham have written '*cleverest*'?

[1] It may be noted that the sentiments attributed to Mrs. Oldfield are but an echo of those of 'Lady Brumpton' in Steele's 'Funeral,' 1701, a comedy in which Mrs. Oldfield had herself taken a minor part. Mme. de Sévigné, who objected to the Provençal method of burying with the hair dressed, and with the addition of a 'Fontange' or 'Commode,' would not have agreed with Narcissa; 'Cela sent le paganisme!' she said. (Faguet's 'Sévigné,' p. 180.)

William Pitt,' says the Master of Peterhouse, 'this was the spirit which dictated them.'[1]

Pitt, Chesterfield, and Lyttelton, it has been said, were inmates of Cobham's temple of Friendship; and it is probable that some of the poet-frequenters of Stowe, especially if they belonged to the Leicester House faction, or shared the principles of the 'Boy Patriots,' followed in their train. James Hammond, who was one of the Prince of Wales' equerries, certainly visited at Stowe, since he died there in June 1742. He refers specifically to the place in one of his imitations of Tibullus:

> To Stowe's delightful scenes I now repair,
> In Cobham's smile to lose the gloom of care,—

the 'care' being presumably that unrequited passion for an obdurate Neaera-Delia (Miss Kitty Dashwood) which was supposed to have shortened his life—either metaphorically or actually. In either case, although he died young, dissolution must have been dilatory, since there are ten years between the completion of his 'miserabiles elegos' and the date of his consequent decease. Another guest and Leicester House adherent, mentioned by Horace Walpole, was Richard Glover, the

[1] 'Globe' 'Pope,' p. 235 n.

first books of whose deep-mouthed and liberty-vaunting epic of 'Leonidas' were inscribed to Cobham; and whose opportune ballad of 'Admiral Hosier's Ghost' made Vernon's capture of Porto Bello at once a whip for the Prime Minister and a spur to the popular hatred of Spain. This latter performance, indeed, which survived the epic, and found its way into the second volume of Percy's 'Reliques,' was actually composed at Stowe.

Hammond was the protégé of Chesterfield, who prefaced his posthumous poems. But after Pope, the greatest of the Stowe minstrels was Thomson, whose particular patron was Lyttelton. In the earlier versions of 'The Seasons' there is no mention of Stowe; but when, about 1743, the author was revising that work, he not only inserted in 'Winter' passages relating to Chesterfield and the recent death of Hammond, but added to 'Spring' a long description of Hagley (Lyttelton's Worcestershire home), and to 'Autumn,' a corresponding glorification of Stowe, couched in terms which imply personal acquaintance both with its beauties and its inhabitants. 'Oh ! lead me,' he exclaims to its garden gods,

> Oh! lead me to the wide extended walks,
> The fair majestic paradise of Stowe.

Not Persian Cyrus on Ionia's shore
E'er saw such sylvan scenes; such various art
By genius fired, such ardent genius tamed
By cool judicious art; that, in the strife,
All-beauteous Nature fears to be outdone.

References to the temple of Virtue, the Elysian Fields, the 'enchanted round' (Bridgeman's walk ?) all point to an experimental knowledge of the locality, while there is express record of prolonged conversations with Pitt, and of the magnetism of the

pathetic eloquence that moulds
The attentive senate, charms, persuades, exalts,
Of honest zeal the indignant lightning throws,
And shakes corruption on her venal throne.

The closing lines, as is fitting, are devoted to the host:

While thus we talk, and through Elysian vales
Delighted rove, perhaps a sigh escapes:
What pity, Cobham! thou thy verdant files
Of ordered trees shouldst here inglorious range,
Instead of squadrons flaming o'er the field,
And long embattled hosts! when the proud foe,
The faithless vain disturber of mankind,
Insulting Gaul, has roused the world to war;
When keen, once more, within their bounds to press
Those polished robbers, those ambitious slaves,
The British youth would hail thy wise command,
Thy tempered ardour and thy veteran skill.

In 1743 'insulting Gaul' had been, or was soon to be, badly beaten by George II. at Dettingen; and for Field-Marshal Lord Cobham, at seventy-four years of age, although there were still honours, there could be little of arboriculture save the 'hated cypresses' of an older bard than Thomson.[1] Lord Cobham died in September 1749. Pope's quatrain, and part of his lines on Stowe, were duly transferred to the fluted column designed by James Gibbs to his lordship's memory, a column which not only testifies to his civil and military exploits, but adds that 'elegantiori Hortorum cultu His primum in agris illustrato Patriam ornavit.' This, surmounted by a statue, was erected by Lady Cobham, who survived her husband until 1760. How long she continued to live at Stowe is not stated; but in the days of Gray's 'Long Story,' she was domiciled at the Manor House, Stoke Poges, which had belonged to her father, Edmond Halsey of Southwark. As Lord Cobham had no issue, the estate of Stowe reverted to his sister Hester, widow of Richard Grenville of Wotton-

[1] 'Neque harum, quas colis, arborum
Te praeter invisas cupressos
Ulla brevem dominum sequetur.'
('Hor.,' ii, 14.)

Underwood in Bucks, who was promptly created Countess Temple. She died in 1752, and was succeeded by her eldest son, Richard. Her only daughter, also Hester, became the wife of William Pitt the Elder, and her second son, George, was Prime Minister to George III. Of the monument of another son, Thomas, the heroic captain of the 'Defiance,' an account has already been given; and of the remainder of the 'mob of nephews,' in Walpole's disrespectful words, nothing more need be said. Earl Temple survived his Prime Minister brother, but dying childless in 1779, Stowe passed to that brother's eldest son George, who later became Marquess of Buckingham and married Mary Nugent, the daughter of Goldsmith's Lord Clare, by his third wife. With the Marquess of Buckingham we enter the nineteenth century, and cross the limits of our chronicle of Stowe.

Whether Hester, Countess Temple, is responsible for any additions to the house or grounds, is not apparent. Her tenure of the place only lasted three years. Her son, Earl Temple, continued to carry out his uncle's designs, several of which had been originally planned by Kent. Such, for example, was the temple of Concord and Victory, an exact reproduction of the beautiful Roman relic at Nîmes known popularly as the Maison Carrée. Cobham's copy was completed in 1763, when it was made to serve as a memento of the English victories of the Seven Years' War—victories which were profusely illustrated by appropriate medallions. Other buildings were the Ladies' temple, also devised by Kent and eventually dedicated to Queen Charlotte; the Gothic temple; the Palladian bridge, a reproduction of that of Inigo Jones at Wilton; the Doric arch in honour of the Princess Amelia, and the memorials to Cook and Wolfe. The former, dated 1778, stood on an islet in the Grotto River; the latter was in the Park, and bore the motto from Virgil which Gladstone later applied to Arthur Hallam, 'Ostendunt terris hunc tantum Fata.' To the matter-of-fact reader, it may seem that the place must have looked a little like an over-monumented cemetery; and indeed something of the kind is hinted by Horace Walpole, when, perhaps remembering the Greek aphorism, he said paradoxically in 1753 that 'half as many buildings, I believe, would be too many; but such a profusion gives inexpressible richness.' A later visitor, Mrs. Lybbe Powys, speaking in 1775, is less ambiguous: 'The buildings [she writes] used, I know, to be thought too numerous, but in such an extent I do not think even that, and the fine plantations now grown up to obscure them properly, must add infinitely to many picturesque views of porticoes, temples, &c., which when originally were expos'd at once, with perhaps three or four more seen from the same point, must have had a very different and crowded effect.' In regard to 'extent,' it must be explained that Stowe was larger than Kew Gardens by more than one hundred acres; and. as Mrs. Lybbe Powys notes, the circuit of the grounds was 'a five-mile walk.' Even Walpole allows that the vastness pleased him more than he could defend.[1]

He had been at Stowe on several occasions between 1753 and 1785, evidently with mixed feelings of interest in the spot and distaste for its owner—to say nothing of his own mutability of temperament. Naturally he was on the side of the landscapists, though he ridiculed the premature commemoration of living notabilities. 'I will not,' he writes, 'place an ossuarium in my

[1] M. Pierre-Jean Grosley, of 'Londres,' who apparently went to Stowe in 1765 on the invitation of Lord Temple, mentions in his account one or two objects omitted in the above list, as Vanbrugh's pyramid, the fountain of Helicon, etc. At this date the Rotundo was occupied by a statue of Venus, and not, as later, by one of Bacchus (1771, iii, pp. 491-502).

garden to my cat, before her bones are placed in it'—a palpable hit at certain significant changes in the tenants of the temple of Friendship. But for many of the buildings he had a genuine admiration. The temple of Ancient Virtue he calls 'glorious.' 'This,' he says, 'I openly worship.' And, as might be expected from the Abbot of Strawberry, he was enraptured with the Gothic 'pastiche,' parcel-Gothic though it were. 'In the heretical corner of my heart I adore the Gothic building, which by some unusual inspiration Gibbs has made pure and beautiful and venerable. The style has a propensity to the Venetian or mosque Gothic, and the great column near it [presumably the Cobham pillar, from which you could see into four counties] makes the whole put one in mind of the Place of St. Mark.' But his best account of Stowe is contained in the letter to Montagu referred to at the outset of this paper, written when he went with the Princess Amelia to visit Lord Temple.

The party consisted of Her Royal Highness, an affable and talkative 'grande dame,' then in her sixtieth year; two of her ladies-in-waiting, Lady Ann Howard and Mrs. Middleton; that pragmatic 'poseuse' and royalty-hunter, Lady Mary Coke; Lord Bessborough, and Walpole.

PRINCESS AMELIA'S ARCH AT STOWE

(FROM THE ENGRAVING BY THOMAS MEDLAND)

Some of their diversions have already been described. But the main object of the expedition must have been to renew the Princess's acquaintance with the Doric Arch which specially concerned her. Walpole's picture of this is in his best manner: 'The chief entertainment of the week, at least what was so to the Princess, is an arch, which Lord Temple has erected to her honour in the most enchanting of all picturesque scenes. It is inscribed on one side "AMELIAE SOPHIAE AUG. [MDCCLXVII]," and has a medallion of her on the other. It is placed on an eminence at the top of the Elysian Fields, in a grove of orange-trees. You come to it on a sudden, and are startled with delight on looking through it: you at once see, through a glade, the river winding at the bottom; from which a thicket rises, arched over with trees, but opened, and discovering a hillock full of hay-cocks, beyond which in front is the Palladian bridge, and again over that a larger hill crowded with the castle [of Stowe]. It is a tall landscape framed by the arch and the over-bowering trees, aud comprehending more beauties of light, shade, and buildings, than any picture of Albano I ever saw.'[1]

'Between the flattery and the prospect,' he

[1] Toynbee's 'Walpole's Letters,' vii, 1904, 393.

goes on, 'the Princess was really in Elysium; she visited her arch four or five times every day, and could not satiate herself with it. The statues of Apollo and the Muses stand on each side. And then follows one of Walpole's verse tributes to the great lady's gratification. A week later comes the reverse of the medal. He is feeling twinges of gout and his retrospect is losing its rose-colour: 'I am come back very lame [he tells Lord Strafford], and not at all with the bloom that one ought to have imported from the Elysian Fields. . . . . It made me laugh as we were descending the great flight of steps from the house to go and sup in the grotto on the banks of Helicon: we were so cloaked up, for the evening was very cold, and so many of us were limping and hobbling,[1] that Charon would have easily believed we were going to ferry over in earnest.'

Three days later he is in bed, reposing not

[1] Elsewhere he says: 'The Earl, you know, is bent double, the Countess very lame, I am a miserable walker, and the Princess, though as strong as a Brunswic lion, makes no figure in going down fifty stone stairs. Except Lady Ann—and by courtesy Lady Mary, we were none of us young enough for a pastoral.' (Toynbee's 'Walpole's Letters,' vii, 1904, 392.)

'under his laurels,' but 'his own tester,' and reflecting ruefully that he should die of fatigue if he were 'to be Polonius to a Princess for another week. Twice a day we made a pilgrimage to almost every heathen temple in that province that they call a garden, and there is no sallying out of the house without descending a flight of steps as high as St. Paul's. . . . To crown all, because we live under the line, and that we were all of us giddy young creatures, of near threescore, we supped in a grotto in the Elysian Fields, and were refreshed with rivers of dew and gentle showers that dripped from all the trees. . . . Not but, to say the truth, our pagan landlord and landlady were very obliging, and the party went off much better than I expected.' If, as he says, he had no delight 'in the Seigneur Temple,' he liked Lady Temple; and had already printed some of her poems at the 'Officina Arbuteana.'[1]

The 'flight of steps,' here twice mentioned, serves to conduct us at last from Stowe Gardens to Stowe House. To be precise, there were not fifty steps, as Walpole says, but thirty-one, and they were flanked at the base by pedestals bearing lions copied from those in the Villa Medici at

[1] 'Poems' by Anna Chamber, Countess Temple, Strawberry Hill, 1764.

Rome. Thence they ascended to a portico or loggia of six lofty Corinthian pillars supporting a pediment. To left and right of this central portion extended colonnades, ending in pavilion wings, the whole presenting a magnificent frontage of more than nine hundred feet, freely decorated with columns, statues, and medallions. This is the aspect which the south-east or garden front presents in Thomas Medland's print of 1797; and in general, it differs little from modern photographs. The north-west view, or park façade, is less impressive. There is a second portico with four Ionic columns and a shorter flight of steps; and from this sweep out two circular colonnades, enclosing a wide gravelled space. The construction of the entire building must have extended over a long period. The middle part was probably built first; a conjecture supported by Celia Fiennes, who, writing under William and Mary, speaks of going from Thornton to see the new house of 'Sr Richd Temple.'[1] This was the first of that name. Sir Richard Temple, the second (Lord Cobham), is said to have rebuilt the façade, and added, or added to, the wings. The original architect is nowhere distinctly named—most likely it was Vanbrugh. Throughout the entire

[1] 'Through England on a Side Saddle,' 1888, 22.

eighteenth century one hears of continual additions and alterations, or the completion of decorations. When Mrs. Lybbe Powys visited the place in 1775, reconstruction was still going on; and the house was surrounded by scaffolding. This was in Earl Temple's day; and further changes were made by the Marquess of Buckingham. Writing ten years later to Conway, Walpole continues to criticise fresh developments, and to comment on modifications in the wings.

To the attentive student of the excellent plan and views which are contained in Seeley's charming little quarto of 1797, dedicated floridly to George Grenville Nugent Temple, Marquess of Buckingham, the first thought will probably be

> 'Thanks, sir,' cried I, ''tis very fine,
> But where d'ye sleep, or where d'ye dine?
> I find, by all you have been telling,
> That 'tis a house, but not a dwelling.'

Swift's biting lines on Blenheim certainly apply in a sense to Stowe, as they do to other eighteenth-century mansions. Spacious 'rooms of state' abound; but the living accommodation is starved proportionately. All along the garden front are vast reception chambers. To left and right of the great oval saloon entered from the portico, with its splendid processional frieze, its choice statues, and its Carrara marble pavement, these apartments open into each other to the farthest extremity of the wings; while on the northern side is a hall corresponding to the portico, and decorated by Kent with a ceiling which celebrates the martial exploits of Lord Cobham. There is a chapel wainscoted with cedar carved by Grinling Gibbons, and having a roof to match that of the Royal Chapel at St. James's; there are a library and ante-library filled with more than ten thousand volumes, chiefly collected by the Marquess of Buckingham; there is a 'Grenville Room'[1] crowded with family portraits, some of them by Reynolds and Kneller, others by that clever amateur, the Marchioness. The great billiard room is filled with miscellaneous portraits, Van Dycks and Lelys and Gainsboroughs. In the dining and drawing rooms and state closet are famous Rembrandts and Rubens's, Claudes and Poussins, Titians and Leonardos, Dürers and Metzus. In other rooms are Gobelin tapestries —triumphs of Bacchus and Ceres, triumphs of the Allies in the Low Countries under Marlborough: and everywhere there are busts, and

[1] Seeley's account of 1797 is here followed. In the Stowe auction catalogue of 1848 the rooms are differently named and disposed.

bronzes, and vases, and tables in 'verde antico'; sphinxes and sarcophagi; chests inlaid with mother of pearl and cunningly carved chimney-pieces; lustres and pier-glasses; green damask and crimson velvet; 'china and old Japan infinite.'

Such was 'eighteenth-century Stowe.' Seen through the fine Corinthian arch at the north end of the two-mile avenue leading from Buckingham, the garden-front still presents to the latter-day spectator much the same aspect as it presented to his predecessor of a hundred years ago. But most of the valuable contents of the house enumerated above, together with other treasures added by later owners, were dispersed in the time of the second Duke of Buckingham and Chandos, at the great sale of 1848, which lasted forty days, and realized more than seventy-five thousand pounds.[1] After the death of the third and last Duke, Stowe House was leased to the Comte de Paris, who died there in September 1894. It belongs at present to the last Duke's daughter, the eighth Baroness Kinloss.

[1] 'Stowe Catalogue,' by H. R. Forster, 1848. The Library and Manuscripts were sold separately in 1849.

ROBERT LLOYD

ON the afternoon of Tuesday, 24th May 1763, Boswell, for whose praiseworthy particularity we can never be sufficiently thankful, paid his first formal visit to Dr. Johnson at his Chambers in Inner Temple Lane. The incidents of this interview, which followed hard upon Boswell's presentation to his new friend in Davies' back-parlour, are sufficiently familiar. But as a preparatory 'wind-up' (in the sense of the elder Weller) to the altitude of the more important business to come, Boswell had taken the precaution of spending the morning in the stimulating society of a little company of wits—'Messieurs Thornton, Wilkes, Churchill and Lloyd.' Wilkes, whose squinting portrait, sketched by Hogarth in Westminster Hall, was at this date only a few days old in the print shops; and Churchill, probably already meditating his retributory Epistle to the painter—require no introduction. Bonnell Thornton, late of the 'Connoisseur,' was speedily to delight the visitors to Ranelagh with his burlesque of the Antient

British Musick—that 'Ode on St. Caecilia's Day,' the Jews' harp and salt-box accompaniment to which so hugely tickled the unmusical ear of Johnson. The fourth of the group, Robert Lloyd, the editor of the 'St. James's Magazine,' is less known. His brief career, soon to end prematurely in the Fleet prison, needs no Trusler to moralize its message. But his fate, deserved or undeserved, conveniently illustrates that lamentable 'Case of Authors by Profession or Trade' which, not many years earlier, Fielding's colleague, James Ralph, had submitted to the consideration of an indifferent public.[1]

Lloyd's father, Dr. Pierson Lloyd, whom Southey describes not only as 'a humourist,' but as 'a kind-hearted, equal-minded, generous, good man,' occupied honourably for some seven and forty years the posts of usher and second master at St. Peter's College, Westminster, otherwise Westminster School. His son Robert, born in 1733, was admitted as a Queen's scholar in 1746, being then thirteen. Among his contemporaries were William Cowper, Charles Churchill, George Colman the Elder, Richard Cumberland, Warren

[1] Ralph's arguments were, in many respects, subsequently enforced by Goldsmith's 'Enquiry into the Present State of Polite Learning in Europe.'

Hastings and Elijah Impey. Another of his intimates in later life was Bonnell Thornton, who, in 1743, had been elected from Westminster to Christ Church, Oxford. During the first year of his school-days, the fifth form usher was that delightful, irresponsible, and indolent Vincent Bourne, so many of whose 'Poematia,' human and modern through all their elegant Latinity, Cowper, fondly ranking his old master with Tibullus and Ovid, was afterwards to render into excellent English. Young Lloyd had marked abilities; and speedily became a more than respectable classical scholar. In 1751, he was captain of the school; and figured at the head of those elected to Trinity College, Cambridge. Of his university studies, there is little record; and his life, remote from the parental eye, is said to have been extravagant and 'irregular.' But he had already shown a bias towards verse. As early as 1751 he had written a long poem in the Spenserian stanza, entitled 'The Progress of Envy,' dealing allegorically with Lauder's attack on the originality of Milton; and he must also have acquired some precocious reputation as an exceptionally fluent versifier, since, in 1754, Cowper addressed to him an Epistle in which, himself writing in octosyllabics, he hails his old schoolfellow as

sole heir, and single,
Of dear Mat Prior's easy jingle;

and even goes as far as to give him the praise, if not of superior finish, at least of superior facility.[1]

While Lloyd was still at Trinity, Thornton and Colman established the weekly paper known as the 'Connoisseur,' one of the brightest and most entertaining of the mid-century Essayists. Not many of its occasional writers are now known; but Cowper certainly assisted, and so did Lloyd. Lloyd's first attempt, in May 1755, was an Epistle to a friend 'about to publish a Volume of Miscellanies,' in which, as introductory to some colloquial characterization of the leading models and a paradoxical commendation of Hawkins Browne's 'Pipe of Tobacco,' he warns his correspondent not to let his verse,

[1] Lloyd was sensible enough to disclaim this too friendly commendation. He knew he had not, as Johnson says of Butler and Prior, the 'bullion' of his model; and he frankly recognizes the fact in a later epistle on 'Rhyme':

'Here, by the way of critic sample,
I give the precept and example.
Four feet, you know, in ev'ry line
Is PRIOR's measure, and is mine;
Yet Taste wou'd ne'er forgive the crime
To talk of mine with PRIOR's rhyme.'

as verse now goes,
Be a strange kind of measur'd prose;
Nor let your prose, which sure is worse,
Want nought but measure to be verse.
Write from your own imagination,
Nor curb your Muse by Imitation,
For copies shew, howe'er exprest,
A barren genius at the best.

Another piece pleads urgently for some revolt against the depressing domination of the pedantic dullard. Not that its writer despises the great legislators of Parnassus:

Although Longinus' full-mouth'd [1] prose
With all the force of genius glows; . . .
Though judgment, in Quintilian's page,
Holds forth her lamp for ev'ry age;
Yet *Hypercritics* I disdain,
A race of blockheads dull and vain,
And laugh at all those empty fools,
Who cramp a genius with dull rules,
And what their narrow science mocks
Damn with the name of Het'rodox.

Two of his remaining contributions are fables; and there is an imitation of a Vauxhall song which effectively reproduces what Mrs. Riot in

[1] In No. 125 of the 'Connoisseur' ('British Classicks,' 1788, vol. vi), quaintly enough, this is printed 'foul-mouthed.'

Garrick's 'Lethe' would call the 'very Quincetence and Emptity' of that popular form of art. The last paper has a prose introduction, dated from 'Trin. Coll. Can., June 6 [1756];' and contains a passage which may perhaps be regarded as autobiographical. Speaking of the Abuse of Words, the writer says: 'I myself, Sir, am grievously suspected of being better acquainted with Homer and Virgil than Euclid or Saunderson [the blind Professor of mathematics]; and am universally agreed to be *ruined*, for having concerned myself with Hexameter and Pentameter more than Diameter.' From which, whatever significance be attached to the word 'ruined,' it may fairly be inferred that he shared with some greater men their distaste for mathematics. And if we are to believe Cowper, there had been too much classics and mathematics at Westminster, and too little religious instruction.

When, in September 1756, 'Mr. Town' of the 'Connoisseur' bade farewell to his public, he made due acknowledgment of the assistance he had received from his Cambridge contributor. According to Welch's 'Alumni Westmonasterienses,' Lloyd 'took the two degrees in Arts in 1755 and 1758.' But, apart from his literary pursuits, his university career, as we have said, had been unsatisfactory, and there was little likelihood of his obtaining a fellowship. To bring him once more under domestic supervision, his father, now second master, obtained for him the post of usher at his old school, a post for which, as far as scholarship was concerned, he was, naturally, abundantly qualified. That the deadening drudgery of the life would not appeal to him, may perhaps be anticipated; and one remembers the heartfelt outbursts of Goldsmith on this particular topic.[1] In Lloyd's 'Author's Apology,' afterwards printed at the head of his collected poems, he dwells bitterly on his memories:

—Were I at once impower'd to shew
My utmost vengeance on my foe,
To punish with extremest rigour,
I could invent no penance bigger
Than using him as learning's tool
To make him Usher of a school;

the duties of which office, he says,

but ill befit
The love of letters, arts, or wit. . . .
Better discard the idle whim,
What's *He* to *Taste*? or *Taste* to *Him*?

---

[1] 'Bee,' 1759, No. vi; 'Vicar of Wakefield,' 1766, ch. xx.

For me, it hurts me to the soul
To brook confinement or controul;
Still to be pinion'd down to teach
The syntax and the parts of speech;
Or, what perhaps is drudging worse,
The links, and joints, and rules of verse;
To deal out authors by retale
Like penny pots of *Oxford* ale;
—Oh! 'Tis a service irksome more
Than tugging at the slavish oar.

Yet such *his* task, a dismal truth,
Who watches o'er the bent of youth;
And while, a paltry stipend earning,
He sows the richest seeds of learning,
And tills *their* minds with proper care,
And sees them their due produce bear,
No joys, alas! his toil beguile,
His *own* lies fallow all the while.

He admits that, before him, both Samuel Wesley and Vincent Bourne had contrived to double the parts of usher and author; but pleads his incapacity to do likewise. Consequently, it was not long before he resigned his position; and, to his prudent father's distress, threw himself on letters for a livelihood.

Granted his aversion from the calling which had been thrust upon him, it must be confessed that his desire to essay a more congenial, if more hazardous career, was not unintelligible. He had many friends in the writing world. Already, at Cambridge, he must have become a member of the select little 'Nonsense Club' of old Westminsters which met weekly for literary purposes combined with conviviality. Of these, Cowper, who by this time had been called to the Bar, was one. Another was Cowper's lifelong friend, Joseph Hill, that 'honest man, close-button'd to the chin, Broad-cloth without, and a warm heart within,' of whom he subsequently wrote.[1] Then there were Bonnell Thornton and Colman, for whom he worked on the 'Connoisseur,' and Bensley, to whom from Cambridge he had addressed two epistles. From one of these it is clear that even in 1757, he had no illusions as to the traditional perils of a literary life:

> You say I shou'd get fame. I doubt it:
> Perhaps I am as well without it.
> For what's the worth of empty praise?
> What poet ever din'd on bays?
> For though the Laurel, rarest wonder!

---

[1] Hill's unmarried sisters, Theodosia and Frances, figure as the 'Modern Antiques' of Miss Mitford's 'Our Village.' According to Southey, they were inveterate sightseers, and supplied an illustrative note to Goldsmith's 'Essays' by sitting up all night for the Coronation of George III.

May screen us from the stroke of thunder,
This mind I ever was, and am in,
It is no antidote to famine.
And poets live on slender fare,
Who, like Cameleons, feed on air,
And starve, to gain an empty breath,
Which only serves them after death.

It is quite possible that the Epistle from which these lines are taken—lines the truth of which their writer was later to illustrate in his own person—was one of the Thursday contributions to the proceedings of the 'Nonsense Club.' But the only other pieces traditionally connected with it which survive, have a different origin. In August 1757, Walpole had 'snatched' from Dodsley, as the first-fruits of the private press at Strawberry Hill, 'two amazing Odes' by Gray, subsequently entitled 'The Progress of Poesy' and 'The Bard.' 'They are Greek, they are Pindaric, they are sublime!' wrote the enraptured Horace to his correspondent Mann; but 'consequently,' he added, 'I fear a little obscure'—an obscurity which, at first, Gray loftily refused to dispel. Under pressure, he appended four short notes to 'The Bard'; but declared he would not have put another for 'all the owls in London.' His epigraph, '*φωνᾶντα συνετοῖσι*'—'vocal to the intelligent'—was, he insisted, 'both his Motto and Comment.' This being so, it is perhaps not unreasonable that the perplexed recipients of a dark saying should complain that it was hard to comprehend; and the first readers of the Odes, Goldsmith among the rest, undoubtedly so complained. In 1760, following the 'Critical Review' by filling up Gray's motto with a qualifying clause which he had purposely withheld,[1] namely—'but, for the generality, requiring interpreters,' Lloyd and Colman set themselves light-heartedly to burlesque 'The Progress of Poesy' by an 'Ode to Obscurity,' and Mason's 'Ode to Memory' by an 'Ode to Oblivion.' The former is sometimes attributed to Colman; the latter to Lloyd; but on either side they were both admittedly 'written in concert.' Here is the first strophe of the 'Ode to Obscurity':

> Daughter of Chaos and old Night,
> Cimmeriam Muse, all hail!
> That wrapt in never-twinkling gloom canst write,
> And shadowest meaning with thy dusky veil!

---

[1] In 1768, when James Dodsley reprinted Gray's poems, the author at last condescended, with subacid contrition, to add some explanatory notes, which include an analysis of 'The Progress of Poesy.' He also, in the circumstances, completed his original epigraph, the latter clause being then relevant.

What Poet sings, and strikes the strings?
It was the mighty Theban spoke.
He from the ever-living Lyre
With magic hand elicits fire.
Heard ye the din of Modern Rhimers bray?
It was cool M[*aso*]n: or warm G[*ra*]y
Involv'd in tenfold smoke.

At this date it is needless to quote more. The parodies are certainly clever; they successfully reproduce some of the poet's peculiarities, as, for instance, his liking for compound epithets, and they could only have been written by scholars. But Gray's unrivalled Pindaric Odes are still babbled by schoolboys 'in extremis vicis,' while the caricatures of Lloyd and Colman, notwithstanding Southey's fantastic proposal that they should form a standing appendix to their models, have now to be sought for in charitable anthologies. Meanwhile, it is interesting to note with what diversity of welcome they were received by Gray's contemporaries. To Warburton they were but miserable buffoonery; to Walpole (friend of both Gray and Mason) 'trash, spirted from the kennel.' On the other hand, Johnson, who preferred Gray's life to his Muse, would have agreed with Southey. 'A considerable part' of the 'Ode to Obscurity' might, he declared, 'be numbered among those felicities which no man has twice attained.' It was the better of the two, he told Boswell on another occasion; but they were both good. 'They exposed a very bad kind of writing.' As for Adam Smith's 'canard,' that Gray was so much hurt 'that he never afterwards attempted any considerable work,' the latter assertion is obviously incorrect, while the former is not supported by Gray's correspondence. Where Gray understands his assailant, he agrees that his assailant 'makes very tolerable fun with him,' though he thinks there is more anger with Mason (to whom he is writing). Elsewhere he says of Colman, then the reputed sole author, 'I believe his Odes sell no more than mine did, for I saw a heap of them lie in a Bookseller's window, who recommended them to me as a very pretty thing.' It is only fair to add that Colman and Lloyd afterwards very frankly recanted to Joseph Warton; and that one of Lloyd's most ambitious Latin imitations was a version of the 'Elegy.' He also specially refers to Gray in his Epistle to Churchill:

> What Muse like GRAY's shall pleasing pensive flow,
> Attemper'd sweetly to the rustic woe?
> Or who like him shall sweep the Theban lyre,
> And, as his master, pour forth thoughts of fire?

When the 'Nonsense Club' was first established is not apparent, nor is it clear when it broke up, though Southey supposes that its dispersion followed upon the defection of Cowper a year or two later. But almost concurrently with the burlesque Odes, to be exact, a few weeks before, Lloyd had issued, in the form of an address to Bonnell Thornton, his first considerable poem, 'The Actor,' an effort of which the 'Gentleman's Magazine' affirmed that 'the Poetry would have pleased, even without the Sentiment, and the Sentiment without the Poetry.' It is, in truth, the most serious of Lloyd's efforts. Its heroics, for he deserts on this occasion his usual octo-syllabics, are neatly wrought; it wisely avoids the criticism of living people by name, paying only careful compliments to Garrick; and it lays its finger upon several obvious stage errors. In action it upholds nature as opposed to tradition; puts (with the late M. Coquelin) the modulation of the voice before excessive gesture, and condemns those popular starts and attitudes which Goldsmith had just been ridiculing in his 'Chinese Letters.'[1] Further, it deplores the 'vile stage-custom' which 'drags private foibles on the public scene,' a palpable hit at Foote, and censures generally over-acting, tricks of dress,

[1] 'Public Ledger,' March 21, 1760.

ghosts, and the absurd entertainments of pantomime. Finally, it takes leave with a graceful lament over the perishable character of the histrionic art:

Yet, hapless Artist! tho' thy skill can raise
The bursting peal of universal praise,
Tho' at thy beck Applause delighted stands,
And lifts, Briareus-like, her hundred hands,
Know, Fame awards thee but a partial breath!
Not all thy talents brave the stroke of death.
Poets to ages yet unborn appeal,
And latest times th' Eternal Nature feel.
Tho' blended here the praise of bard and play'r,
While more than half becomes the Actor's share,
Relentless death untwists the mingled fame,
And sinks the player in the poet's name.
The pliant muscles of the various face,
The mien that gave each sentence strength and grace,
The tuneful voice, the eye that spoke the mind,
Are gone, nor leave a single trace behind.

Cibber's 'Apology' is credited with the germinal form of this somewhat self-evident truth. In 1766, half-a-dozen years later, Garrick compressed it into a well-known couplet of his Prologue to the 'Clandestine Marriage';[1] and Sheridan, with much facile 'fioriture,' included it in that

[1] Nor Pen nor Pencil can the Actor save;
The Art, and Artist, share one common Grave.

'Monody' which was spoken by Mrs. Yates at Drury Lane, on the great actor's death. But it was Lloyd who first elaborated the idea. Its latest form, as regards the vocalist, is to be found in de Musset's admirable 'Stances à la Malibran.'

With Lloyd's judicious commendation of the autocrat of Drury Lane must no doubt be connected the performance, at that theatre, of his Ode on the death of George II, entitled the 'Tears and Triumph of Parnassus,' 1760, to be succeeded, in the following year, by the dramatic pastoral of 'Arcadia; or, the Shepherd's Wedding,' in honour of the august nuptials of Charlotte of Mecklenburg-Strelitz and George III. Both of these occasional, and nowise remarkable, productions had the advantage of the music of John Stanley, the blind organist of the Temple Church. Lloyd also supplied Garrick with several prologues: for the King's birthday; for Colman's 'Jealous Wife' (in which he seems to glance at the author's obligations to Fielding's 'Tom Jones'); and for the 'Hecuba' of Miss Burney's eccentric Brighton friend, Dr. John Delap. But the most definite and important outcome of 'The Actor' was, unquestionably, 'The Rosciad' of Charles Churchill. Disqualified for a university career by an early and imprudent Fleet marriage,

Churchill, by 'need, not choice,' had been leading a precarious life on the 'forty pounds a year' of a country living, eked out by tuition. In 1758, at his father's death, he had been elected, by favour of the parishioners, to the curacy and lectureship of St. John the Evangelist, Westminster. Dr. Pierson Lloyd, his former master, had helped him more than once in money difficulties, as Churchill afterwards acknowledged,[1] by mediating with his creditors; and Robert Lloyd, unhappily for himself, was also warmly attached to his old class-mate. The favourable reception of 'The Actor' roused the dormant faculties of Churchill, whose first metrical essays were unfortunate. A Hudibrastic poem called 'The Bard' was declined by the booksellers as worthless; a second, 'The Conclave,' satirizing the Dean (Dr. Zachary Pearce) and Chapter of Westminster, was regarded as too libellous for publication. But in these tentative efforts, Churchill had found his strength; and for a fresh subject he selected the Stage, in which he had always been interested. 'After two months' close attend-

[1] Dr. Lloyd was the 'kind good man' of 'The Conference,' who,

'Image of him whom Christians should adore,
Stretch'd forth his hand, and brought me safe to shore.'

ance on the theatres,' he completed 'The Rosciad.' Even for this he was refused the trifling fee of five guineas. Thereupon he boldly issued the poem at his own expense.

The result in the theatrical world has been aptly compared to that caused by the discharge of a gun in a rookery. Churchill being utterly unknown, the anonymous writer was at first supposed to be Lloyd, assisted possibly by Thornton and Colman; but apart from the fact that one of the most serious passages in the piece, a plea for the moderns against the ancients, is placed in Lloyd's mouth, the ascription showed little critical acuteness. There was no resemblance whatever between Lloyd's easy generalities and the direct cudgel-play of his more fearless friend. Such lines as

> He mouths a sentence, as curs mouth a bone,

which is said to have driven Davies from the boards to the book-shop; the remorseless

> PRITCHARD'S for Comedy too fat and old;

and the

> MOSSOP, attach'd to military plan,
> Still kept his eye fix'd on his right-hand man,

were, compared with Lloyd, as the roaring of the

tiger to that of the sucking dove; and neither the dove nor the tiger was at first particularly pleased by the turn which things had taken. Churchill, however, in the second edition, openly claimed the authorship: and, in a shorter poem entitled 'The Apology,' proceeded, with an energy which left no doubt as to his staying power as a satirist, to trounce his chief assailant, the 'Critical Review,' then edited by Smollett; while Lloyd's affectionate and unenvious nature speedily forgot its own annoyance in admiration for the superior gifts of his friend—gifts to which, moreover, he paid admiring homage in more than one epistle:

Pleas'd I behold superior genius shine,
Nor ting'd with envy wish that genius mine.
To CHURCHILL's muse can bow with decent awe,
Admire his mode, nor make that mode my law;
Both may, perhaps, have various pow'rs to please:
Be his the Strength of Numbers, mine the Ease.

Elsewhere, in 'The Poet,' Lloyd draws Churchill's portrait with all the fervency of friendly enthusiasm:

Is there a man, whose genius strong
Rolls like a rapid stream along,
Whose Muse, long hid in chearless night
Pours on us like a flood of light,
Whose acting comprehensive mind
Walks Fancy's regions, unconfin'd;

Whom, nor the surly sense of pride,
Nor affectation, warps aside;
Who drags no author from his shelf,
To talk on with an eye to self;
Careless alike, in conversation,
Of censure, or of approbation;
Who freely thinks, and freely speaks,
And meets the Wit he never seeks;
Whose reason calm, and judgment cool,
Can pity, but not hate a fool;
Who can a hearty praise bestow,
If merit sparkles in a foe;
Who bold and open, firm and true,
Flatters no friends—yet loves them too:
CHURCHILL will be the last to know
His is the portrait, I would show.

By 'The Rosciad' and 'The Apology' Churchill made more than a thousand pounds, with which, to his credit, he paid his debts. But at this stage, discarding first his clerical garb for gold lace and ruffles, and next, for he resigned his cure, his clerical character, he unhappily embarked with all the ardour of a vigorous constitution, upon those pleasures of the town which, in the measured words of Gibbon, 'are within the reach of every man who is regardless of his health, his money, and his company.' Into the train of this worst of Mentors, Lloyd, docile and unstable, was only too readily drawn; and people who were still smarting from the strokes of Churchill's criticism, were not slow to comment upon such unworshipful developments of literary success. As may be imagined, the tale lost nothing in the telling; and it is quite conceivable, as suggested by William Tooke, the earliest editor of Churchill, that irregularities which, in some of his contemporaries, would have passed unnoticed, or been indulgently condoned as mere eccentricities of genius, were magnified by the victims of his pen into acts of unbridled depravity. More thin-skinned than most satirists—which is saying a good deal—Churchill bitterly resented this inquisition into his 'midnight conversations'; and, in a poem called 'Night,' addressed to Lloyd, endeavoured to defend himself against his traducers. But his defence, based upon the then-current fallacy that honest vices are more excusable than hypocritical virtues—as if, says a modern critic, there were no possible third course—is not convincing; while it seems besides to indicate incidentally that the 'sons of CARE,' as they curiously styled themselves, did not always derive from their dissipations the distraction they sought. Nor is the later apology of their boon-companion and evil-genius, Wilkes, drawn speciously from the precedents of antiquity, any more to the point. Of Wilkes, however, we may safely say, 'Non tali auxilio'; and, moreover, we are not writing, nor design to write, a paper on Churchill, being, for the present, busied only with his friend Lloyd.

Lloyd, unlike Churchill, had not found verse a monetary success; and although he never at any time overcame his rooted antipathy to tuition, he must also have soon discovered that one form of servitude was no better than another; and that by octo-syllabics, however easily they jingled, it was difficult to live. His prologues and theatrical pieces can have produced but little. For some months previous to the appearance of 'Arcadia,' he had been acting as editor of the poetical department of 'The Library,' a periodical conducted by Dr. Andrew Kippis, later to be better known as projector of an interrupted 'Biographia Britannica.' Lloyd's connection with 'The Library' lasted until May 1762, when he issued a quarto volume of 'Poems' including 'The Actor,' the Epistle to Churchill, the Burlesque Odes, and a number of minor pieces. From the lengthy list of subscribers,[1] it would

[1] Besides the 'great vulgar and the small,' many notable names appear in its columns. Not to mention Henry Fox and Charles Townshend and Richard Owen Cambridge,

seem that this collection should have been the most lucrative of his publications; but although he appears to have always performed his daily task with mill-horse regularity, it is clear that his gains, as a man of wit, never sufficed to his expenditure as a man of pleasure, and that from the outset he was embarrassed. With September 1762 he issued the first number of the 'St. James's Magazine,' Davies being one of the publishers. Of course it was to be like nothing else. It was to deal exclusively with Belles Lettres. It was to be original and various; it was to be scholarly; it was to be soundly critical. The hackeyed attractions of the ordinary monthly

there is 'Mr. Samuel Johnson' (he was not yet Doctor); there are 'William Hogarth, Esq;' (to whom Lloyd had addressed a laudatory epistle concerning 'Sigismunda'), and Messieurs Reynolds and Wilson, 'Painters'; there is the sculptor, Roubillac. There are Newbery and Dodsley, booksellers; there are those curious clergymen, the Rev. Charles Churchill and the Rev. Laurence Sterne; there are Garrick and Foote, and Cowper and Akenside, and the two Wartons, and Laureate Whitehead. For Gray and Mason and Horace Walpole it would be idle to seek. Whether all the names meant money, it is hard to affirm. Six months later, the book was still announced in the 'St. James's Magazine' as 'just published'; and Kenrick, Lloyd's editor, says in 1774 that a remainder had been 'lately disposed of at an inconsiderable value.'

were to be studiously avoided. It would contain

> No pictures taken from the life,
> Where all proportions are at strife;
> No Humming-Bird, no painted Flower,
> No Beast just landed in the Tower,
> No wooden Notes, no colour'd Map,
> No Country-Dance shall stop a gap; . . . .
> No Crambo, no Acrostic fine,
> Great letters lacing down each line;
> No strange Conundrum, no invention
> Beyond the reach of comprehension,
> No Riddle, which whoe'er unties,
> Claims twelve Museums for the Prize,
> Shall strive to please you, at th' expence
> Of simple taste, and common sense.

Some of these promises were kept, but even in the first number there was departure from the programme, inasmuch as its final pages were occupied by an account, 'lifted' bodily from the 'London Gazette,' and certainly not Belles Lettres, of the great event of 1762, the taking of the Havannah from the Spaniards, with other occurrences, Foreign and Domestic. As usual, the editor had many disappointments from the 'eminent hands' who had promised their assistance. Churchill, whose fast-following productions were, with copious extracts, rapturously reviewed, sent nothing; and Garrick is only represented by a prologue and epilogue. On the other hand, Cowper contributed an ironical 'Dissertation on the Modern Ode'; and also, it is supposed, a subsequent exemplification of it, though this is initialed 'L,' and may have been by Lloyd.[1] From the introductory remarks, Cowper, it would seem, had contemplated an Art of Poetry on the same plan; but his intentions were prevented by that second derangement to which belong those terrible Sapphics beginning 'Hatred and vengeance, my eternal portion.' From Falconer of 'The Shipwreck' came 'The Fond Lover' a song 'written at sea,' and dated 'Royal George'; from Christopher Smart, a eulogistic epitaph on Fielding, and a fable.[2] Bonnell Thornton sent,

[1] Southey thought it by Cowper, and Mr. H. S. Milford, though not without hesitation, includes it in his excellent Oxford edition of that poet, pp. 288-9. The form resembles Mason's, and it is possible that the following lines are obliquely aimed at him:

> 'Come placid DULLNESS, gently come,
> And all my faculties benumb,
> Let thought turn exile, while the vacant mind
> To trickie words, and pretty phrase confin'd,
> Pumping for trim description's art,
> To win the ear, neglects the heart.'

[2] One of the occasional contributions (which must have issued from the shades) consists of two Greek epigrams by

among other things, some specimens of an intended translation of Plautus, being portions of the 'Miles gloriosus,' a task to which he had been stirred by emulation of Colman's Terence. Colman again, copying Lloyd's own epistle from the Cobbler of Tissington to Garrick, pens a companion letter to Lloyd himself, in which, with great good humour, and no little truth, he rallies his old schoolfellow for trusting overmuch to his metrical facility. He warns him that if he 'cramps his Muse in four-foot verse,' he will ultimately find 'his ease his curse.' Why does he not 'write a great work! a work of merit'? Otherwise,

> Too long your genius will lie fallow
> And ROBERT LLOYD be ROBERT SHALLOW.

The advice was more easy to give than to take, especially by an editor whose contributors were voluntary; and who, in their default, was pledged to fill five sheets per month with printed

Fielding's 'Parson Adams,' then the *late* Rev. William Young of Gillingham. Another writer adapts to the memory of Shenstone, who died in February 1763, his own epitaph—the 'most beautiful of epitaphs,' Landor calls it—on his cousin, Maria Dolman—'Ah! Gulielme, Vale! "Quanto minus est, Cum aliis versari, Quam tui meminisse."'

matter, and that matter more verse than prose. No wonder Lloyd was weary of the task, and had already written:

> Continual plagues my soul molest,
> And *Magazines* disturb my rest,
> While scarce a night I steal to bed,
> Without a couplet in my head,
> And in the morning, when I stir,
> Pop comes a *Devil,* 'Copy, sir.'
> I cannot strive with daring flight
> To reach the brave *Parnassian* HEIGHT,
> But at its foot, content to stray,
> In easy unambitious way
> Pick up those flowers the muses send,
> To make a nosegay for my friend.

One of his most assiduous colleagues, a certain equally facile but forgotten rhymer, Mr. Charles Denis, who was a brother of the famous admiral and patron of Thackeray's 'Denis Duval,' furnished translations of La Fontaine, Marmontel, Voltaire, Boileau and other versions or paraphrases from the French. Lloyd himself padded his pages with a long prose rendering of the 'Nouvelle École des Femmes' of M. Moulier de Moissy, his ostensible pretext being to show to what extent Churchill's enemy, Arthur Murphy, had relied upon that comedy for his own piece, 'The Way to Keep Him.' There are also ominous proposals for a complete translation of Racine, to be published as a monthly make-weight. Lloyd seems to have struggled doggedly with his 'métier de forçat,' for he says in his general Preface to vol. i, that he is personally responsible for upwards of seven hundred lines in every number; but it cannot be denied that he is often open to the charge of being 'shallow.' He nevertheless shows constant capabilities for better things. One of his dialogues, 'Chit-chat,' is a bourgeois paraphrase of the 'Two Ladies of Syracuse' in Theocritus. A Cheapside Gorgo and Praxinoë, Mrs. Brown and Mrs. Scot, go (in their sacks and cardinals) to see, not the Adonis festival, but that memorable contemporary show, the opening of Parliament by George III, with the gingerbread splendours of whose state-coach, recently designed by Chambers the Architect, they are duly impressed. The close imitation of an original demands a certain restraint, which was good for Lloyd; and though it is not easy to select a quotation, 'Chit-chat' is a very satisfactory specimen of his better manner. But long before the 'St. James's Magazine' had reached its closing blue numbers, that ill-fated serial was plainly, in its projector's words, dragging out

a miserable being,
Its end still fearing and foreseeing;

and when, in February 1764, the long-threatened end came, Lloyd had for some time surrendered the work to other hands, and was himself, 'for debts contracted during its progress,' an inmate of the Fleet.

What his liabilities were we know not; but they need not have been large. In those days, in spite of Oglethorpe's Committee, a beneficent legislature still permitted a vindictive creditor to seize the body of an unhappy debtor for a trifling sum, casting him into a custody from which he might never again emerge;[1] and, as we know from Johnson's 'Rambler,' the Fleet, the King's Bench and the other prisons, were at this date crowded with many such miserable captives, who were exposed to all the discomforts arising from dirt, disease, foul air, bad food, and the grinding rapacity of tyrannical keepers. Why Lloyd, whose father was still a master at Westminster

[1] But I have also heard a sweet Bird sing,
That Men, unable to discharge their Debts
At a short Warning, being sued for them,
Have, with both Power and Will their Debts to pay,
Lain all their Lives in Prison for their Costs.
FIELDING'S *Pasquin*, 1736.

School, was suffered to remain for a moment in such a degrading environment, may perhaps be explained by the supposition that, freed by one claimant, he would only be arrested by another; and that, while he remained in the Fleet, or the limits known as its Rules or Liberties, he could not be arrested at all. Churchill, on hearing of his incarceration, at once hastened to his assistance, and provided for his immediate wants by supplying him with a servant and a guinea a week. This sum (unless it was spent as promptly as the similar allowance made to Richard Savage) should have sufficed to save Lloyd from the squalors of 'Mount-scoundrel,' and to secure him decent food and lodgment. Churchill also attempted to set on foot a subscription for his eventual release. But from mismanagement, or other causes now too obscure to make intelligible, the proposals came to nothing; and Lloyd remained in durance, receiving numerous visitors, though apparently abandoned by most of his old associates. 'I have many acquaintances,' he wrote mournfully to Wilkes in France, 'but now no friends here. He continued to drudge hopelessly for the booksellers, finishing a version of Klopstock's 'Death of Adam'; translating, with Charles Denis, Marmontel's 'Contes Moraux'; and endeavouring to console himself philosophically by the reflection that irksome as confinement was, it was 'not so bad as being usher at Westminster.' He even produced 'The Capricious Lovers,' a little comic opera from the French of Favart's 'Ninette à la Cour,' which Garrick accepted for Drury Lane. On 4th November 1764 Churchill, who in his 'Independence'[1] made indignant reference to Lloyd's continued confinement, ended his own meteoric course at Boulogne, where he died of fever. The rest may be told in Southey's words: 'Lloyd had been apprised of his [Churchill's] danger; but when the news of his death was somewhat abruptly announced to him as he was sitting at dinner, he was seized with a sudden sickness, and saying, "I shall follow poor Charles," took to his bed, from which he never rose again; dying, if ever man did, of a broken heart. The tragedy did not end here: Churchill's favourite sister, who is said to have possessed much of her brother's sense and spirit and genius, and to have been betrothed to Lloyd, attended him during his illness; and, sinking under the double loss, soon followed her brother and her lover to the grave.'

[1] 'Hence, Ye vain Boasters, to the *Fleet* repair,
And ask, with blushes ask, if LLOYD is there.'

When Robert Lloyd was buried in the churchyard of St. Bride's parish he was thirty-one, and his premature end is sad enough. At the same time, it is impossible to give to the tale of his misfortunes more than the commiseration usually conceded to those who, in common parlance, are 'nobody's enemy but their own.' The record of his personality is scant and indistinct. He is said to have been modest, affectionate, generous, and devoted to those he liked. Truth constrains us to add that he was also weak-willed, fond of pleasure, and easily led away by companions whose social gifts were not ballasted with more solid merits. As a poet, either from lack of ambition, or from a conscious sense of limitation, he never fulfilled the promise of his youth. He was a sound scholar, without the least touch of pedantry; he had a fertile fancy, considerable humour, and an excellent judgment. The too-ready fluency on which he so much relied was nevertheless unfavourable to 'fundamental brain-work'; and the pressure of necessity frequently hurried him into reckless over-production. Hence, in a short paper, it is difficult to borrow from his work more than a few autobiographical and literary passages. His melancholy story exemplifies most of those ills which his great contemporary had gloomily declared to be the allotted portion of letters:

> Toil, Envy, Want, the Patron and the Jail.

But he was spared the Patron.

GRAY'S BIOGRAPHER

CONNECTED with Mason's 'Memoirs of the Life and Writings of Gray' is one of those odd freaks of circumstance by which the whirligig of Time occasionally diverts the philosophic inquirer. Dr. Johnson was a Tory; Mason was a Whig—therefore Johnson did not like Mason. Johnson, moreover, did not like Gray, whom, in conversation, he bracketed with Mason as inferior to Akenside; and this was another reason why he was prejudiced against Mason's biography of Gray. Consequently, one is not surprised to learn that, though he forced himself to read the book because it was 'a common topick of conversation,' he found it 'mighty dull.' 'As to the style (he added), it was fit for the second table'—a figure of disparagement which is included, though not explained, in Dr. Birkbeck Hill's list of 'Dicta Philosophi.' But the piquant point about the great man's judgment is, that it was this very life of Gray by Mason which Boswell made his model for what Macaulay has called, on this occasion without contradiction, the first of all biographies. 'I have resolved,' says Boswell in his introductory pages, 'to adopt and enlarge upon the excellent plan of Mr. Mason in his Memoirs of Gray'—in other words, to intersperse the text with letters which exhibit the man. 'I am absolutely certain,' he had already written to his friend Temple, 'that my mode of biography, which gives . . . a *view* of his [Johnson's] mind in his letters and conversations, is the most perfect that can be conceived.' Thus the book that Johnson found 'mighty dull,' supplied the proximate pattern for Boswell's masterpiece; and as Horace Walpole was not slow to perceive, marked the starting point of a new departure in literary portraiture. While rejoicing—for Walpole too had views on style—that the 'Memoirs' did not imitate 'the teeth-breaking diction of Johnson,' he wrote on its first appearance in 1775 that 'its merit did not depend on the competence of the present age.' 'You have,' he told Mason, 'fixed the method of biography, and whoever will write a life well must imitate you.' Walpole's precept and the practice of Boswell fairly justify some brief parley with that now occulted 'Person of Importance in his Day'—Gray's biographer.

For, although in our time the Rev. William

Mason, Rector of Aston and Precentor of the Cathedral Church of St. Peter in York, is almost entirely forgotten, in his own he was undoubtedly a 'person of importance.' Even Hartley Coleridge, who has written of him at large in the 'Northern Worthies,' more, it is to be suspected, because he came within the scheme of that Boreal Biography than from any special admiration for his character and achievement, is constrained to admit that, besides being the friend and biographer of Gray, he was, at the time of writing, 'the most considerable poet that Yorkshire had produced since Marvell,' and the hundred-page estimate winds up with the statement that 'for many years of his life he was England's greatest living poet.' This latter, to be sure, is not saying much, though it is difficult to dispute it. Mason was a placid, amiable, well-educated man, and also a highly-respectable specimen of the comfortably-beneficed ecclesiastic of that apathetic Georgian epoch, when, it has been said, little remained in the larger part of the English Church but 'a decorous sense of duty and a sleepy routine of practice.' His clerical functions left him ample leisure for 'Shakespeare and the musical glasses'; and his literary tastes secured him the friendship of Gray and Walpole, of whom he was the diligent correspondent. Without exceptional imagination, he had considerable facility and metrical accomplishment. He wrote elegies and Pindaric odes, tragedies on Greek models with English subjects, satires which are neat but not deadly, and blank verses on gardening—in all of which he 'neither sinks nor soars.'[1] Most of his work is difficult reading now, although we know one septuagenarian who remembers studying 'Caractacus' in his boyhood with romantic interest; and we have little doubt that ladies of quality once wept as freely over 'Elfrida' as did Lady Hervey over Home's 'Douglas' or Lady Bradshaigh over Richardson's 'Clarissa.' But it would need complicated hydraulics to extract a solitary tear of sensibility from the present generation. *Autres temps, autres pleurs!*

However this may be, the 'rural Pan' of the period (doubtless a Pan in a Periwig!) appears to have 'breathed' benignly on the 'helpless cradle' of the future author of 'The English Garden.'

[1] Mason himself professed to claim no more than this:

'So, through life's current let me glide,
Nor sink too low, nor rise too high,
Safe if Content my progress guide,
And golden Mediocrity.'

But we must not take modesty too much at its word.

Mason's father, the Vicar of Holy Trinity in Kingston-upon-Hull, where, in 1724, Mason was born, not only personally superintended his education, but fondly fostered his bias towards verse-writing and painting—a course which, Hartley Coleridge observes, made it unnecessary for him to add 'the curse of disobedience to the calamities of poetry,' and which, in his twenty-second year, he dutifully acknowledged in heroic couplets. At St. John's College, Cambridge, where he was entered in 1743, he found a congenial tutor in Dr. Powell, who, besides directing his attention to classic models, encouraged him in cultivating what Thomas Warton calls 'the warblings of the Doric oate.' Other Cambridge friends were his uncle, Dr. Balguy, and later, Hurd, afterwards Bishop of Worcester. His first model was Milton; and his earliest essays, 'Il Bellicoso' and 'Il Pacifico,' published years afterwards in the first volume of Pearch's 'Miscellany,' were obviously prompted by 'L'Allegro' and 'Il Penseroso.' A more ambitious performance, 'Musaeus, a Monody to the Memory of Mr. Pope,' was a professed imitation of 'Lycidas.' This, Gray, then living at Cambridge, was, by the good offices of a friend, induced to revise, although he was as yet unknown to the author; and on Dr. Powell's advice it was published by Dodsley in April 1747. It had no small success, and passed into a third edition. To the reader of to-day, in spite of the neatness of the versification, it will seem a rather mechanical 'melodious tear': but, it may be admitted that the poet shows a certain originality by making Milton, Chaucer, and Spenser visit Pope, 'in the trance preceding his departure,' for the purpose of assuring him of their own poetical unworthiness. This they do in character. Chaucer, the Tityrus of the deputation, thanks Pope for making his 'sely rymes,' 'ren right sote.' Milton, its Thyrsis, addresses him Miltonically in sonorous blank verse; while Spenser (Colin Clout), after the fashion of M. Edmond Rostand, borrows the imagery of his stanza from the farmyard:

Like as in village troop of birdlings trim,
Where Chanticleer his red crest high doth hold,
And quacking ducks, that wont in lake to swim,
And turkeys proud, and pigeons nothing bold;
If chance the peacock doth his plumes unfold,
Eftsoons their meaner beauties all decaying,
He glist'neth purple and he glist'neth gold,
Now with bright green, now blue himself arraying.
Such is thy beauty bright, all other beauties swaying.

To which Pope replies in a valedictory allocution which shows that Mason could also successfully echo the Popesque note. Whether, as his critic maliciously suggests, the speakers' mode of speech be, or be not, studied from Pope's paraphrases rather than the originals, these imitations certainly serve to explain why, in after years, Mason was so quick to decide on the fictitious element in Chatterton's Rowley poems.

According to Mr. Ralph Straus's recent life of Dodsley, the reception of 'Musaeus' made Mason anxious to undertake the task, afterwards so liberally performed by Thomas Warton, of editing Milton's Minor Poems. 'I have often thought it,' he writes, 'a great pitty that many of the Beautiful Peices it [the "3rd vol. of Milton"] contains shou'd be so little read as they certainly are, I fancy this has arisen from the bad thing they are tack'd to [?]. I want vastly to have a seperate edition of the Tragedy, Mask, Lycidas & Lallegro, &c.' But Tonson, to whom the copyright belonged, proved intractable, and the idea came to nothing. Meanwhile, early in 1748, Dodsley brought out the first three volumes of his 'Collection of Poems by Several Hands,' in the last of which he reprinted 'Musaeus' (with a ridiculous illustration by Frank Hayman); and included a fresh piece by Mason, an 'Ode to a

Water-Nymph.' With this arises Gray's first written reference to Mason, who was seven years his junior: 'Mr. Mason [he writes from Stoke to Dr. Wharton of Durham] is my Acquaintance. I liked that Ode very much [the ode just mentioned], but have found no one else, that did. he has much Fancy, little Judgement, & a good deal of Modesty. I take him for a good & well-meaning Creature; but then he is really *in Simplicity a Child*, & loves everybody he meets with: he reads little or nothing, writes abundance & that with a design to make his fortune by it.' [1]

Mason had the courage to reprint this not entirely flattering picture in his later 'Memoirs' of Gray, remarking only on the last words that, at the period referred to, he was, in truth, 'perfectly well satisfied if his publications furnished him with a few guineas to see a play or an opera.' But evidently he did not share Gray's nervous horror of being paid for his productions. As regards the 'Ode to a Water-Nymph,' it may here be noted that Dodsley's version closes with a laudation of Lyttelton and Lyttelton's eloquence, of the beauties of Lyttelton's seat at Hagley, and

[1] Tovey's 'Letters of Thomas Gray,' 1900, i, 178. This extract illustrates Gray's employment and neglect of capitals, as also his use of the ampersand.

of the monody on the death of his charming first wife, which had come out in Dodsley's second volume. All this was afterwards suppressed, and the poem 'concluded according to the Author's original idea'—a proceeding for which no explanation is vouchsafed, though it is easy to suggest one. Whether Mason was already acquainted with Lyttelton does not appear. But if, as stated by Mr. Courtney[1] in his attractive little study of Dodsley's collection, most of the pieces it contained were submitted to Lyttelton before they were 'passed for printing,' nothing would be more natural than that it should occur, or should even be suggested by Dodsley, to one of the contributors that an opportunity might be found for gracefully flattering a distinguished statesman and patron of letters. And Mason, if not a strikingly original thinker, was quite acute enough to anticipate and act upon the worldly-wise injunction of Martin Routh of Magdalen: 'Attach yourself to some great man, Sir! Many have risen to eminence in that way.'

Gray's letter to Wharton is dated 5th June 1748; and in another to Walpole he speaks of his new friend's 'Musaeus' as seeming 'to carry

[1] 'Dodsley's Collection of Poetry: its Contents and Contributors.' By W. P. Courtney, 1910, p. 2.

with it a promise at least of something good to come.' In 1745 Mason had taken his B.A., and quitted St. John's with a valedictory Ode to Dr. Powell. In the following year a second Ode commemorated his expectation to return to Cambridge, since, chiefly on the recommendation of Gray, he had been nominated to a Fellowship in Pembroke Hall. Owing, however, to the opposition of the Master, Dr. Long, he was not elected until early in 1749. In February of the same year he published a monologue entitled 'Isis,' directed against the supposed spirit of Jacobitism prevailing at Oxford, as evidenced by recent disorderly demonstrations amongst the gownsmen in favour of King James the Third. In this the goddess, tearful and dilapidated, or, as her poet puts it, 'in all the awful negligence of woe,' is made to invoke the shades of Sidney and Hampden, of Addison and Locke, to console her for the disloyalty of her seditious sons. The piece was promptly parodied by Byrom, and being also answered with considerable vigour by the future laureate, Thomas Warton, then of Trinity College, Oxford, Mason, perhaps not uninfluenced by a polite reference to 'Musaeus,' had the good sense to admit himself outdone. His next effort was a composition to be set to music, written, at the request of the authorities, for the installation as Chancellor of the University of Cambridge of that egregious personage, Thomas Pelham Holles, Duke of Newcastle, then Secretary of State for the Northern Department in the Pelham Administration. The musician was Dr. Boyce; and it was performed in the Senate House on 1st July 1749; as part of what Gray, making report to Wharton, calls a 'Week of Wonders': 'Every one, while it lasted, was very gay, & very busy in the Morning, & very owlish & very tipsy at Night. I make no exception [he adds] from the Chancellour to Blew-Coat [the Vice-Chancellor's servant]. Mason's Ode was the only Entertainment, that had any tolerable Elegance; & for my own Part, I think it (with some little abatements) uncommonly well on such an Occasion.'

By this time its author is 'growing apace into his good Graces, as he knows him more.' 'He is very ingenious with great Good-Nature & Simplicity. a little vain, but in so harmless & so comical a Way, that it does not offend one at all; a little ambitious, but withall so ignorant in the World & its Ways, that this does not hurt him in one's Opinion. so sincere & so undisguised that no Mind with a Spark of Generosity would ever think of hurting him, he lies so open to

Injury. but so indolent, that if he cannot overcome this Habit, all his good Qualities will signify nothing at all. after all I like him so well, I could wish you knew him.' Some of these 'characteristics of the poetical temperament,' as Chalmers calls them, seem to have adhered to Mason through life; others, it is significantly added, were 'effaced by a closer intimacy with the world.' But from Gray's words, it is clear that Mason was already in a fair way to become the familiar 'Skroddles' of their future correspondence.

That correspondence, nevertheless, did not begin until July 1753, when Gray's first published letter to Mason is dated. In the interval Gray's famous 'Elegy' came out; and in the same letter in which he writes to Walpole of its premature publication, he mentions a play, 'wrote by a person he has a very good opinion of.' He proposes to send Walpole the beginning: 'It is (unfortunately) in the manner of the ancient drama, with choruses, which I am to my shame the occasion of; for, as great part of it was at first written in that form, I would not suffer him to change it to a play fit for the stage, and as he intended, because the lyric parts are the best of it, they must have been lost. The story is Saxon, and the language has a tang of Shakespeare, that suits an old-fashioned fable very well.' In a later letter he tells Walpole that the author and the piece are in town together; and begs for Walpole's observations, engaging not to betray more of his verdict than may be 'fit for the ears of a tender parent,' who, he adds, 'has ingenuity and merit enough (whatever his drama may have) to bear hearing his faults very patiently.' Whether Walpole's criticism was favourable or unfavourable is not recorded; but the play was published by Knapton in March 1752, under the title of 'Elfrida; a dramatic poem, written on the model of the antient Greek Tragedy. By Mr. Mason.'

Prefixed to 'Elfrida' is a sequence of letters in which the author sets forth his attempt to write an English play on Greek lines, a contradiction in conception to which, in spite of all opposition, he continued obstinately attached. Hartley Coleridge discusses these prolegomena, as well as the play itself, with much learning and at considerable length; but it is useless to reproduce here his arguments for or against a work no longer under discussion. The real Ælfthryth or Elfrida, daughter of Orgar, ealdorman of Devonshire, became the second wife of Edgar, king of England. Subsequently, according to William of Malmesbury, she entered upon a wedded career quite discreditable enough to qualify her for the highest walks of Attic tragedy. Mason, however, did not needlessly hamper himself with historical accuracy. He makes Edgar send his minister Athelwold to offer his crown to Elfrida. But Athelwold falls in love with the lady himself; marries her, and hides her—with a convenient chorus of British virgins—in a secluded castle in Harewood Forest. To this retreat she is tracked by her father and Edgar. Athelwold is killed by the king in single combat; and dies murmuring (like Richardson's Lovelace), 'This atones for all.' Thereupon Elfrida promptly gets her to a nunnery. The play contains many careful lyric passages, especially in the choruses; and 'the Shakespearean tang' is often not unskilful. But the primary and fundamental difficulty—the reconciling of English sentimental drama with the atmosphere and machinery of the Greek stage—is not satisfactorily overcome. In book form 'Elfrida' had, notwithstanding, considerable success, but at the date of issue no attempt was made to put it on the boards.[1]

[1] Some of its admirers must have been extravagant enough to satisfy the most exacting literary self-esteem. A rhymer in the 'Gentleman's Magazine' for March 1752—with a profusion worthy of Browning's Italian sonneteer—

Towards the close of 1753, Mason lost the father who had so carefully watched over his boyish studies. From his correspondence with Gray, it would seem that a second marriage had practically deprived him of his paternal estate, and reduced his means to his Pembroke Hall Fellowship. He consequently took orders in 1754; and being fortunate enough to secure a patron in the Earl of Holderness (a Secretary of State), was appointed, not only his domestic chaplain, but was presented to the living of Aston, near Rotherham, in the West Riding of Yorkshire. In the

contrives in six lines to compare Mason to (1) Sophocles, (2) Plato, (3) Pindar, (4) Homer, and (5) Virgil. Then, pausing to regret that his

'noble scenes should stand no chance
With a dull *Pantomime*, or paltry dance!

he goes on to predict that

'ELFRIDA still shall shine, and MASON'S name
Distinguish'd stand in the bright roll of fame,
Till time shall stop, 'till nature's frame decay,
And earth, and sea, and heav'n pass in one blaze away.'

And yet Mason's name is not included in Mr. Humphry Ward's Pantheon of 'English Poets'! Nor—ode-maker as he was—does he gain a place in Mr. Edmund Gosse's anthology of that form; although, of necessity, he finds judicial record in Mr Courthope's monumental 'History of English Poetry.' The lines in the 'Gentleman' are signed 'R. D.' (Query—Robert Dodsley.)

former of these capacities his duties carried him to the Continent, where he met another Cambridge man, William Whitehead, then travelling as governor, or tutor, to Lord Villiers and Lord Nuneham. All three are mentioned in a letter to Gray from Hanover of June 1755, in which Mason regales his correspondent with a burlesque kit-cat of the local librarian (who might have served as a model for Chodowiecki), and an account of a Hamburg lady with the uneuphonious name of Belcht, who had read the 'Elegy' with mild enthusiasm, but was entranced by the 'Nitt Toats' of Young. In March of the following year, reverting to the choric measures with which 'Elfrida' had originated, Mason printed four odes—on Memory, Independency, Melancholy, and the Fate of Tyranny.

It is said that the odes were not well received, and that the tendency of the author to purple epithets and alliterative art was freely criticized. Nevertheless, a second edition followed in April. Of the four pieces named that on Memory is the best, though Gray regarded as 'superlative' a Gray-like couplet in 'Melancholy' ('To a Friend'):

> While thro' the west, where sinks the crimson Day,
> Meek Twilight slowly sails, and waves her banner gray.

'The Fate of Tyranny' is a paraphrase of part of the fourteenth chapter of Isaiah—a task which might well have overburdened even a bolder bard than Mason; and whether 'Independency' is better or worse than Smollett is, as Hartley Coleridge says, no matter. In August 1757 Horace Walpole printed at Strawberry Hill, and Dodsley published Gray's 'Progress of Poesy' and 'The Bard'; after which, in March 1758, Gray's Odes and two of Mason's were included in the sixth and final volume of Dodsley's Collection. How, not long afterwards, both Mason and his friend were assailed by the parodists Lloyd and Colman, has already been related in the preceding paper;[1] and it is only necessary to add now, what was not then stated, that Mason seems to have taken the matter much more to heart than Gray, who, having apparently assimilated Lanoue's precept 'la plainte est pour le sot,' philosophically declined to 'combustle' about it. But Mason had more to lose; for the 'Bard' is still studied, and few have even heard of the 'Ode to Memory.'

By this date, Mason must already have been far advanced with 'Caractacus,' another and more ambitious dramatic poem 'on the model of

[1] See 'Robert Lloyd,' pp. 220-2.

the ancient Greek tragedy,' for Gray is already criticizing some form of it in December 1756; and by September of the next year has read over the MS. twice 'not with pleasure only, but with emotion.' 'The contrivance, the manners, the interests, the passions, and the expression go (he considers) beyond the dramatic part of "Elfrida" many leagues'; and he proceeds to devote one of the longest of his letters to close criticism of the details. 'Caractacus' was published in May 1759, and deals with the story of that King of the Silures who, taking sanctuary with the Druids in Anglesea, was afterwards captured and sent to Rome. The Chorus, still a salient feature of Mason's plan, is composed of Druids and Bards. The background is one that lends itself to impressive landscape painting; the fable is stronger; the characterization more firm; and the lyric parts more finished than in 'Elfrida.' Indeed, it would not be difficult to make quotations, could they be more than dislocated fragments. But the insuperable difficulty remains, that, however effective as a dramatic poem, 'Caractacus,' like its predecessor, is no more an acting play than, according to Sir Arthur Pinero, is Browning's 'Blot in the 'Scutcheon.' In 1772 Colman brought out an adapted 'Elfrida,' against the author's will, threatening him, when he expostulated, with a chorus of Grecian washerwomen. Mason afterwards altered it himself; and it was again performed, without success, in 1776. A somewhat better fate attended the concurrent production of 'Caractacus,' but even that never obtained any permanent place on the stage.[1]

After 'Caractacus,' Mason's next publication was a shilling pamphlet of three elegies issued by Dodsley in December 1762, though dated 1763. Two of these, the elegy 'Written in the Garden

[1] Walpole's opinion of 'Caractacus' was not as favourable as Gray's. 'Mr. Mason [he tells George Montagu in June, 1759] has published another drama, called 'Caractacus'; there are some incantations poetical enough, and odes so Greek as to have very little meaning. But the whole is laboured, uninteresting, and no more resembling the manners of Britons than of Japanese.' On the other hand, the 'Biographia Dramatica' is almost as hysterical as Mr. Urban's critic of 'Elfrida.' Conceding that 'Caractacus' was never intended for the English stage, 'in the closet'—it goes on—'it lays the strongest claim to immortality, and is one among a few instances, that poetical genius is so far from its decline at this time in these realms, that we have writers now living, some of whose works no British bard whatsoever, Shakspeare, Spenser and Milton not excepted, would have reason to blush at being the author of.'

of a Friend' (Robert Wood, the author of 'Palmyra' and 'Baalbec'), and that 'On the Death of a Lady' (Maria, Lady Coventry), which was so great a favourite with Rogers—are among his best efforts in this kind. Another Elegy, not included in the trio, and inscribed to Dr. Hurd, then rector of Thurcaston in Leicestershire, figures as a dedication to 'Caractacus.' Here Mason develops his dramatic purpose. His desire, he says, had been to persuade the tragic Muse of Sophocles, with her 'golden lyre' and 'buskin'd pomp,' to bring to Britain her 'choral throng,' and 'mingle Attic art with SHAKESPEARE's fire.' To which the Muse replies oracularly:

> Mistaken suppliant, know,
> To light in SHAKESPEARE's breast the dazzling flame
> Exhausted all PARNASSUS could bestow.
> True; Art remains; and, if from his bright page
> Thy mimic power one vivid beam can seize,
> Proceed; and in that best of tasks engage,
> Which tends at once to profit and to please.

In 1764 these pieces, with all his previous poems, except the 'Isis' and the 'Installation Ode' (which latter was probably withheld because the author had got nothing out of 'Old Fobus,' as he and Gray profanely called the Duke of Newcastle), were collected in one volume. The former reference to Lyttelton in the 'Ode to a Water Nymph' was withdrawn,[1] Mason having now a practicable patron in Lord Holderness, to whom the book was dedicated, and who, besides giving him the Aston living and helping to procure him a chaplainship to George II, had recently obtained for him the precentorship of York Cathedral. This, with a York residentiary canonry, which he owed to another friend, Frederick Montagu, increased his means by about £400 per annum, so that his hunger for advancement—his 'insatiable repining mouth,' Gray called it—if not satisfied, should, for the moment at least, have been appeased. The next important occurrence in his life was his marriage on 25th September 1765,[2] to Miss Mary Sherman of Kingston-upon-Hull, a beautiful and amiable young woman, to whom he seems to have been genuinely attached. His happiness, however, was of brief duration. Mrs. Mason proved consumptive, and in spite of sedulous nursing, died at the Bristol Hot Wells in March 1767, being then twenty-eight. She is

[1] In a letter of June 1760 Gray speaks of Lyttelton as 'your old patron,' so that, at some time, Mason must have had hopes from that quarter.

[2] An extract from the register of St. Mary Lowgate was communicated to 'Notes and Queries' in October 1881 by the late Arthur Munby.

buried in the north aisle of Bristol Cathedral under an epitaph composed by her husband which, like most of Mason's work, has been praised and dispraised. By one modern critic of distinction it is frankly denounced as 'fustian'; but the popular voice—influenced probably by the occasion—is in its favour.[1] Mason's own part of it, the first twelve lines, may be conventional enough;[2] but the beauty of the final quatrain, contributed by Gray, who also wrote an admirable letter to his bereaved friend, would be sufficient to efface far better lapidary work than Mason's:

Tell them, though 'tis an awful thing to die,
  ('Twas ev'n to thee) yet the dread path once trod,
Heav'n lifts its everlasting portals high,
  And bids 'the pure in heart behold their God.'

---

[1] A sentimental eighteenth-century admirer, and votary of the 'Sorrows of Werther,' Miss Eliza Dawson of Oxton in Yorkshire, had long cherished the hope of seeing Mason on account of this epitaph. But when her hopes were at last realized, she was dismayed to find him 'a little fat old man of hard-featured countenance,' entirely absorbed in his game of whist. (Paston's 'Side-Lights on the Georgian Period,' 1902, p. 259.)

[2] Of one expression: 'She bow'd to taste the wave,' it is but fair to state that, according to Pearch's 'Miscellany,' 1775, i, 217, Mrs. Mason actually died 'while drinking a glass of the waters.'

Gray says that Hurd objected to the third line. But the imagery is legitimately Biblical, and it is hard to see why objection was raised. In any case, it is fortunate that Mason did not avail himself of Gray's generous permission to 'make another' line in its place if he pleased.

That Mason deeply felt his loss there is no doubt. Although long, in Gray's phrase, 'in a "mariturient" way,' he had been over deliberate in deciding. He was forty when he became a husband, and his wedded life lasted no longer than eighteen months. But it gave him something to think of besides himself; it was his happiest time; and, as Southey says, being happy he was cheerful. After his wife's death, he lapsed again into his old listless habit of discontent—a discontent no doubt intensified by the remembered 'tempo felice.' His chief distraction seems to have been gardening. Already, in the dedicatory sonnet to Lord Holderness prefixed to the poems of 1764, he had referred to this:

> Here, as the light-wing'd moments glide serene,
> I weave the bower, around the tufted mead
> In careless flow the simple pathway lead,
> And strew with many a rose the shaven green.'

He was a fervent adherent of the new landscape school; and for the further solace of his mind began, soon after his wife's death, to work at his most prolonged poetical effort, the 'English Garden,' of which the first book, setting forth the pervading principle, appeared in 1772. The three remaining books, containing practical directions and making some two thousand five hundred lines in all, followed at leisurely intervals, the last appearing in 1782, when an Irish friend, Dr. Burgh, added an elaborate commentary and notes.

Warton, who did not like Mason, nevertheless describes the 'English Garden' as 'didactic poetry brought to perfection by the happy combination of judicious precepts with the most elegant ornaments of language and imagery.' The verdict is a little machine-made; but it was no doubt honest. Hartley Coleridge, writing many years later, thought it 'one of the dullest poems he had ever attempted to read,' and he, obviously was equally in earnest. Which is right? A not unreasonable answer would be 'Both.' Warton was judging the 'English Garden' as an eighteenth century didactic poem. To-day we do not care greatly for didactic poetry, however ingeniously decorated. Yet we should hardly go as far as Hartley Coleridge. Those who are curious in landscape gardening (and there are still a few!); those who love to read of bowling-greens, and

Ha Ha's, and cascades, and hermitages, and the temples of Signor Borra, and the sham ruins of Sanderson Miller, to say nothing of that wise Sidonian king whom Fanny Burney called 'Abdolomine'—might well find their account in Mason's pages. It is true that blank verse offered pitfalls to his taste for redundancy; it is true also that, before the first book appeared, he had lost the patient and judicious critic who had so often pruned his luxuriances and 'castigated' his vocabulary. To this he himself refers in opening Book iii:

> Clos'd is that curious ear, by Death's cold hand,
> That mark'd each error of my careless strain
> With kind severity; to whom my Muse
> Still lov'd to whisper, what she meant to sing
> In louder accent; to whose taste supreme
> She first and last appeal'd, nor wish'd for praise,
> Save when his smile was herald to her fame.

And so forth. Some lines that follow refer to a special memorial which he erected to his friend at Aston. This was a rustic alcove, or summer-house, which contained an urn and medallion portrait of Gray. Over the entrance was a lyre surmounted by the poet's motto from Pindar to his Odes; and below, on a tablet, with slight variation, came one of the discarded stanzas of the 'Elegy':

Here scatter'd oft, the loveliest of the year,
By hands unseen, are showers of violets found;
The red-breast loves to build and warble *here*,
And little footsteps lightly print the ground.

According to Murray's Handbook of Yorkshire for 1904, at that date this historic summer-house was still in existence at Aston, where the garden continued to preserve the old stretches of green-sward, the winding walks between the trees, and the openings which revealed the 'distant blue' of the Derbyshire hills referred to in Mason's last and best anniversary sonnet:

Yet still my eyes can seize the distant blue
Of yon wild Peak, and still my footsteps bold,
Unprop'd by staff, support me to behold
How Nature, to her Maker's mandate true,
Calls Spring's impartial heralds to the view,
The snowdrop pale, the crocus spik'd with gold.

On 30th July 1771, Gray died, and was buried on 6th August in Stoke-Poges churchyard. He left to Mason £500, together with all his 'books, manuscripts, coins, music printed or written, and papers of all kinds, to preserve or destroy at his own discretion.' Out of this bequest Mason began, not long afterwards, to prepare Gray's 'Memoirs.' Borrowing a hint either from his own indolence, or Conyers Middleton's life of Cicero, and discarding the stereotyped method of his day, he proceeded, by printing Gray's letters with a brief connecting narrative and notes, to make him, as far as possible, 'his own biographer,' and in this way to present 'a regular and clear delineation of his life and character.' His plan proved excellent; and it was at once adopted by subsequent writers as the true method of life-writing. It remains the true method of life-writing still—where there are letters, be it understood; but in Mason's case there was one grave defect, of which his contemporaries were happily ignorant. Regarding Gray's correspondence as mere raw material, he treated it in a way which would now be regarded as disingenuous. A biographer is no doubt entitled to suppress or withhold as he thinks fit, but he is not justified in garbling or falsifying. Mason practically did both. He left out passages without indicating that anything had been omitted; he turned two letters into one; and he freely altered the wording in others where he thought alteration was required. He may possibly have held that he was justified in what he did by the custom of his day; and it is not necessary to suppose him wilfully misleading. But he certainly cannot be defended on one plea which has been put forward in his defence, namely—that he could not foresee the future interest which would attach to Gray as an author. The question is one of editorial good faith; and it remains a serious drawback to a work which Rogers read and re-read delightedly; which Miss Mitford regarded as 'one of the most attractive books ever written;' and which, sophisticated though it be, does not give an unfavourable or inadequate picture of Mason's friend and critic.

Little requires to be said of Mason after the appearance in 1775 of Gray's biography. One of the accidents of its preparation was that it brought about a prolonged correspondence with Horace Walpole, only interrupted at last by political differences. The first book of 'The English Garden' also led to the 'Heroic Epistle to Sir William Chambers,' already sufficiently treated in a former collection of these papers,[1] although it may be stated here, as further proof of the extravagant praise which, even when its author wrote anonymously, he received from his contemporaries, that Hannah More regarded it as, both for matter and versification, 'the best satire since the "Dunciad"!' Mason followed up the 'Heroic Epistle' by some minor satirical pieces, which add little to his reputation, even if they

[1] 'Old Kensington Palace, and Other Papers,' 1910, p. 222, *et seq.*

reveal unsuspected power of epigrammatic invective. Beyond dispersed Odes and Sonnets, his chief remaining work was a translation into heroic verse of Du Fresnoy's 'De Arte Graphica,' dedicated to Sir Joshua Reynolds, who annotated it. He also painted Mason's portrait; and, by will, left him Cooper's miniature of Milton.[1] Politics occupied much of Mason's later years, though, besides gardening, he found some time for hobbies such as painting and church music. His musical gifts were fully recognized, and he was one of the favoured persons to whom Dr. Burney presented his book on the 'Present State of Music in France and Italy.' Of his painting, examples are the altar-piece of the 'Good Samaritan' at Nuneham church, and a not-very-pleasing pencil-sketch of Gray at Pembroke College.[2] As

[1] Mason left this to Dr. Burgh, and it is now at Rokeby in the possession of the Morritt family. A letter from Mason to Malone respecting it is printed in Prior's 'Malone,' 1860, p. 193. Although it *is* by Samuel Cooper it is not now held to represent Milton (see Dr. G. C. Williamson on 'The Cooper Miniature' in the 'Catalogue of the Portraits, Prints, and Writings of John Milton,' exhibited at Christ's College, Cambridge, 1908, pp. 17, 80-2).

[2] There is a copy of it in Gosse's 'Works of Gray, 1884, vol. iii.

to politics, the acme of his many glorifications of Freedom and Liberty was a Secular Ode (1788) on the Anniversary of the Landing of King William at Torbay. But the terrible object lesson of the French Revolution proved as disturbing to Mason as to Walpole; and in 1797 he published a shuddering palinode, bidding 'Avaunt!' to 'abhorr'd Democracy.' In April of the same year he died, aged seventy-two. He has a monument in Westminster Abbey, next to Gray, and a tablet in Aston Church.

Both as a writer and a personality Mason is exceedingly difficult to appraise. That much of the simplicity, modesty and amiability with which Gray credited him on their first acquaintance was not permanently done away by subsequent commerce with the world, is quite conceivable; nor is it necessary to doubt that he 'discharged the common offices of life as a man and a clergyman, with a uniform propriety and decorum.' In later life he inherited an estate which brought his income up to £1,500 a year; and of this he is said to have given away a third in 'patronage and charity.' But his correspondence, published by Mitford long after his death, does not exhibit him in an entirely attractive aspect. He praises retirement yet hankers after the 'Cambridge coffee-houses'; he combines the most lofty view of poetry with the keenest eye for the financial results; he courts criticism and finesses to avert it; he preaches 'golden mediocrity' (an ill-chosen phrase!), but is always pushing uneasily for fresh preferment. These after all are only human frailties, though they illustrate the inexpediency of following up 'the full voice which circles round the grave' by the frank disclosure of familiar communications. As to his poetry, we should scarcely now be governed by the 'Gentleman's Magazine' or even the 'Biographia Dramatica'; but when one realizes that he was praised by a Quarterly Reviewer, as late as 1816, for 'metrical epitaphs' that rival Dryden, and 'sonnets' that far surpass Milton, one can only 'stare and gasp.' It is true that the same critic curses as well as blesses, for he credits him (justly) with 'superfluity' and a 'diction florid even to the confines of bombast.' He has sometimes been compared with Gray—and he would not have objected; but any one who cares to make that comparison experimentally has only to take up Dodsley's last volume (which closes with Mason's Odes to Independency and Melancholy followed by Gray's 'Progress of Poesy' and 'Bard') in order to perceive that there is a material difference between the master and the scholar, the difference of genius.[1] Correct, well-equipped, copious, Mason is mainly imitative; and what is best in him he owes to Gray and Gray's criticism. He ranks with those versemen who mistake memory for inspiration, and facility for distinction; who reject living humanity, and rejoice in lifeless personification; whose art, if it sometimes instructs, seldom really moves or elevates. One of his sonnets is addressed to that 'emblem pure of legal liberty,' a 'Gravel Walk.' A great Elizabethan once wrote another to the 'Highway' which—for the nonce—was his 'chief Parnassus.' But there is nothing of the 'gravel walk' about Sir Philip Sidney. There is too much of it in William Mason.

[1] See also the additions which, as he says, he had the 'boldness' to make to Gray's unfinished 'Ode on the Pleasure arising from Vicissitude' ('Poems and Memoirs,' 2nd ed., 1775, pp. 235, 76).

APPENDIX A

Carmontelle's Transparencies

TO the particulars given at pp. 38-9 may be added the following from the French edition of Frénilly's 'Memoirs':

'Who,' writes Frénilly, speaking of Carmontelle, 'has not known his transparencies? It was a charming invention, the most original in the world, and which has been badly imitated since: by means of a band of paper which unrolled itself from one cylinder to roll itself again on another, a picture fifteen inches high by about three feet wide renewed itself continually, presenting to the eye landscapes, towns, monuments, balls, illuminations, conflagrations—a crowd of scenes from life. Carmontelle did several of this sort, and owed it to them that he did not die in the workhouse. For when he saw the conspiracies of his detestable prince [Egalité], he nobly resigned his reader's place by which he lived, and would have died of hunger without asking or complaining if the excellent Duc de Charost, who loved and esteemed him, had not contrived to make him accept an annuity of 4,000 francs as the price of one of his transparencies. In this way his pride was not offended. He was very old, and I do not know if he prized a landscape of Claude Lorraine more than his transparencies. Before leaving this man who so much amused my youth, I must say a couple of words concerning a magic lantern which he exhibited one night at my father's. Contemporary personages were shown in action. Their appearances, costumes, adventures, peculiarities, were all passed in review, and with this, abundance of anecdotes, bons mots, sly hits, and Savoyard buffoonery. This representation, full of wit and taste, is still perfectly visible to me, though it is sixty years since I saw it' ('Souvenirs du Baron de Frénilly,' 1908, p. 8).

The above passage, it will be seen, throws further light on the story of Carmontelle's last days and circumstances. It is also possible that Mme. de Genlis was thinking of this special development of the transparencies when she likened them to 'a sort of magic lantern' (p. 38).

APPENDIX B

Exhibitions of the Eidophusikon

CLEVER Mr. Pyne, masquerading in 'Wine and Walnuts' as Ephraim Hardcastle, shows a curious and censurable coyness in the matter of dates. He carefully refrains from mentioning the year in which he visited the Eidophusikon, described in the twenty-first chapter of his first volume. And thereby arises a difficulty, and hangs a tale. The Eidophusikon is usually supposed to belong to 1781—or thereabouts. But the storm-scene referred to by Pyne represents the loss at Seacombe, in the Isle of Purbeck, Dorset, on Friday, the 6th of January 1786, of the 'Halsewell,' outward bound East Indiaman.[1] The solution is, that there was more than one exhibition of Loutherbourg's 'moving pictures,' and that Pyne was familiar with that of 1786 alone. He was but a boy in 1781, and he professes to speak 'de visu.' In 1786 he was between sixteen and seventeen; and in that year the wreck of the 'Halsewell' was part of Loutherbourg's show.

The 'Eidophusikon' was exhibited for the first

[1] 'Annual Register,' 1786, p. 224.

time on the 26th February 1781;[1] and the place of exhibition, as per advertisement in the public prints of the day, was a large house in Lisle Street, fronting Leicester Street, Leicester Square. The price of admission was 5*s*., and the performance began at seven. It was arranged in five scenes, as follows:

1. AURORA; or, the the Effects of the Dawn, with a View of London from Greenwich Park.
2. NOON; the Port of Tangier in Africa, with the distant View of the Rock of Gibraltar and Europa Point.
3. SUNSET, a View near Naples.
4. MOONLIGHT, a View in the Mediterranean, the Rising of the Moon contrasted with the Effect of Fire.
5. The Conclusive Scene, a STORM at Sea, and Shipwreck.

The Music for the performance was composed by Michael Arne, Dr. Arne's son, who played the harpsichord. Between Scenes 2 and 3 came one of Schubert's sonatas; and there was a musical introduction to the closing picture. There was also between each scene a Transparency. These represented:

1. An Incantation.

[1] The particulars that follow are mainly derived from the 'Public Advertiser.'

2. A Sea Port, a conversation of Sailors of different Nations.
3. A View in the Alps, a Woodcutter attacked by Wolves; and
4. A Summer Evening, with Cattle and Figures.

For Noon (No. 2 Scene) was later substituted a 'topical' new Scene, The Bringing of French and Dutch Prizes into the Port of Plymouth, with a View of Mount Edgecumbe.

After fifty-nine evenings, the first season came to an end in May. On Monday, 10th December, it opened again in the same place, Lisle Street, Leicester Square. Entirely new music was provided by Mr. Burney, who also accompanied the 'Scenes' on the harpsichord, while the 'vocal Part' was undertaken by that favourite singer at Vauxhall and Ranelagh, Mrs. Sophia Baddeley. On 21st December the show closed for the holidays, with promises of fresh attractions, especially a 'conclusive Scene' from Milton. The new Pictures, which were duly exhibited on 31st January, comprised:

1. The Sun rising in the Fog, an Italian Seaport.
2. The Cataract of Niagara, in North America.
3. The Setting of the Sun, after a Rainy Day, with a View of the Castle, Town and Cliffs of Dover.
4. The Rising of the Moon, with a Water Spout, exhibiting the Effect of three different Lights,

with a View of a Rocky Shore on the Coast of Japan.

THE CONCLUSIVE SCENE

5. Satan arraying his Troops on the Banks of the Fiery Lake, with the Raising of Pandemonium, from Milton.

After 7th March, the Storm and Shipwreck scene, which had always been highly popular, was restored 'by particular Desire,' and the performance was divided into Two Acts, the Storm closing the first, and the Miltonic scene the second. As time went on, however, the attendance fell off; and the prices were reduced to 3*s.* and 2*s.* 6*d.* On 31st May the show was closed.

Four years later, on the 30th January 1786, after the wreck of the 'Halsewell' East Indiaman, the Eidophusikon was reopened, the storm scene being modified so as to give an 'exact, awful, and tremendous Representation of that lamentable Event,' a narrative of which, based on the accounts of the chief surviving officers, was to be obtained of William Thomson, the popular bookseller of the Exchange; and for the music and melody of Burney and Baddeley was substituted English Readings and Recitations 'by Mr. Cresswick.' In this way the existence of the exhibition was protracted until 12th May, which was announced as 'positively the last night,' a valedictory 'bonne bouche' being provided by the appearance, 'immediately previous to the Grand Scene from Milton' of the Polish dwarf, Borulwaski, who performed several pieces on the English guitar. Borulwaski, who survived until 1837, must at that date have been nearing fifty, and probably had reached his full height, about 3 ft. 3 in. After 12th May 1786 there is apparently no further mention of Loutherbourg's famous show, and what became of the properties when sold history has not revealed.

APPENDIX C

Death of the Bailli de Suffren

M. JAL'S informant was M. Dehodencq, who died on 12th May 1849, aged eighty-seven, at No. 61, rue du Faubourg-Montmartre, a house in which M. Jal himself lived for forty-one years. He had known M. Dehodencq for thirty years; and had frequently heard his account of the Bailli's death. After the Revolution, Dehodencq became a 'limonadier,' or coffee-house keeper, and for a long period held the café of the Théâtre des Variétés, a favoured resort of literary men. Shortly stated, his story was as follows: In 1788, Dehodencq, then about six and twenty, was a member of the Bailli's household, in the modest capacity of 'officier de la bouche' under the 'Intendant,' Jean-Simon Gérard, father of the François Gérard who afterwards painted the Bailli's portrait. In the month of December, Dehodencq remembered hearing from the Bailli's valet, Duchemin, that his master had been brought home from Versailles with a sword-thrust through the body. By order of a surgeon, who was immediately called in, Dehodencq was sent out to get some nettles in order to 'fouetter,' or 'débrider (stimulate) la plaie,' an operation which had no success. It was winter; and Dehodencq was accustomed to say that he found the nettles under the snow in the allée des Veuves of the Champs Elysées. The particulars preceding the tragedy, as gathered by Dehodencq from those about the Bailli in his last hours, were that he had been importuned by the Prince de Mirepoix to interest himself on behalf of two of the Prince's nephews under punishment for some dereliction of duty in the East Indies. Suffren, a blunt seaman, and by no means prepossessed in favour of the class of 'marins pour rire' to which they belonged, at first remained silent. Being pressed, he replied at last in negative terms so contemptuous as to provoke a challenge, which he accepted, notwithstanding the fact that he was nearly sixty, and as stout as Marshal de Noailles or the 'Gros Duc' d'Orléans. This encounter took place at Versailles, behind Bernini's equestrian statue of Curtius at the head of the Pièce d'Eau des Suisses; and the Bailli, fatally wounded, was carried home to the Hôtel Montmorency to die, which he did in three days, leaving strict injunctions that the circumstances should remain profoundly secret. This account, taken down almost entirely from Dehodencq's dictation, M. Jal published in a note to his 'Scènes de la vie maritime,' 1832, iii, p. 161. On the 17th July 1845, M. Cunat, of St. Malo, then engaged on the Bailli's biography, and wishing to confirm the facts from the witness's own lips, visited Dehodencq at Batignolles, in company with M. Jal. Dehodencq repeated, much in the same terms, what he had formerly related to Jal, adding a few minor details which duly figure in M. Cunat's pages. The story naturally found no very favourable reception with the Bailli's family; and, as might be expected, other versions were put forward. One, preserved by J. S. Roux ('Le Bailli de Suffren dans l'Inde,' 1862, pp. 231-2), makes the duel the result of an altercation at a ball; according to another, dating from 1866, Suffren fell a victim to the mistaken treatment of a physician sent to him by order of Mesdames of France. But verisimilitude and congruity are on the side of M. Jal.

Although M. Cunat deprecates what are known as 'faits privés,' both he and M. Roux supply us with some of the Bailli's traits. In action Suffren's habitual head-dress was a wide-brimmed felt hat, which had been given to him by his brother, the Bishop of Nevers and Sisteron, and which was regarded by the common seamen with as much superstitious veneration as the historical grey coat of Napoleon inspired in the veterans of the Grande Armée. Like Nelson, negligent of his costume, which in India his excessive corpulence obliged him to reduce as much as possible, he generally appeared in his shirt and a light cotton vest or jacket. He resembled Robinson Crusoe in being frequently accompanied by a favourite parrot;

and, as may perhaps be inferred from his obesity, was an excellent trencherman, fully recognizing the sanctity of the dinner-hour. His tastes, nevertheless, were simple. He was warmly attached to his family and friends; and in all his campaigns seems to have sighed for the quiet of his Provençal home. But once on ship-board his energy was indefatigable, and he never yielded to the enervating influence of an Eastern atmosphere. 'Je sers,' he wrote to his friend, the Countess d'Alais, 'pour faire la guerre, non ma cour aux femmes de l'Isle de France.' By the able seaman, who knew his work, the Bailli was idolized; by the 'officier à talons rouges,' who did not, he was naturally disliked. A rigorous disciplinarian, he was inexorable to cases of insubordination or imputed cowardice; and his concise and uncompromising censure, conveyed in a constitutionally nasal tone, must have been an additional terror to delinquents. 'Je persiste,' he said, receiving the excuses of a defaulter, 'je persiste à dire que vous avez entaché le pavillon.' Some of his letters to the Countess d'Alais, published by Captain Ortolan in the 'Moniteur' for 1859, give an intimate idea of his individuality.

POSTSCRIPT

The statement at p. 177 that Dehodencq's story, as related by him to M.M. Jal and Cunat, is 'now generally accepted,' derives its confirmation from the fact that it is repeated in such current works of reference as the dictionaries of Hoefer, Larousse, and Bouillet. But, as it often happens, page 285 had no sooner been returned for press than the writer became aware that another version of the Bailli's death had recently been put forward, not on the side of Dehodencq, but supporting the story of 1866 that the Bailli died of ill-timed blood-letting (' une saignée intempestive'). This story was known to M. Jal. With additional detail, it is retold in the attractive 'Légendes et Curiosités de l' Histoire' by Dr. Cabanès [1912], pp. 255-265: 'Comment est mort le Bailli de Suffren.' Dr. Cabanès quotes M. Lacour-Gayet, a member of the Institute, who cites a little treatise on Gout and Rheumatism by Dr. Alphonse Leroy, published in 1805. Dr. Leroy was the friend and medical adviser of the Bailli. According to this authority, the Bailli had gone to Versailles to visit Madame Victoire, the aunt of Louis XVI. He had been suffering from gouty erysipelas. He looked so ill that the princess proposed to send him her own physician, who prescribed bleeding in the arm. It was objected that the Bailli's medical man had ordered leeches on the feet: 'Le médecin de cour, rapporte le docteur Leroy, répondit par un petit sarcasme. M. de Suffren, impatienté, offrit le bras; mais à peine fut il piqué, qu'après un peu de sang épanché, il perdit connaissance; la goutte fit une métastase rapide sur la poitrine. On réitéra la saignée, et lorsque j'allai voir cet illustre ami, qui m'avait promis de se faire appliquer les sangsues aux jambes, je restai stupéfait en apprenant son agonie . . .' (p. 264). This account, it is but right to state, was not penned to refute the duel story, but is an 'obiter dictum' in a medical work—a fact which adds to its value as evidence. On the other hand, one remembers Jal's first question to Dehodencq in 1845: 'D'abord, dites moi, je vous prie, le Bailli est bien mort d'apoplexie, n'est-ce pas?—Non, non, en duel! Et en disant ces mots, M. Dehodencq a vivement porté la main sur son cœur, comme pour affirmer sur l'honneur la vérité de ce qu'il disait.' It is difficult to conceive why Dehodencq, for no appreciable motive, should have invented and persisted in the circumstantial story which carried conviction to the minds of MM. Jal and Cunat. Meanwhile, it may be noted that the interesting volume of Dr. Cabanès contains an excellent copy of Houdon's bust of the Bailli in the Musée d'Aix.

GENERAL INDEX

N.B.—*The titles of articles are in capitals*

Abdalonymus, 267.
Aboukir Bay, Landing at, Loutherbourg's, 124.
Actor, Lloyd's, 223.
Adhémar, Count d', 52.
Admiral Hosier's Ghost, Glover's, 196.
A FIELDING "FIND," 128-149.
Akenside, Mark, 243.
Alembert, Jean le Rond d', 87.
Alexandria, Battle of, Loutherbourg's, 124.
Algarotti, Francis, 82, 83.
Allaire, Abbé, 60.
Allen, Mrs., 5, 13, 14.
Alms, Captain James, 169.
Amelia, Fielding's, 26, 128.
Amelia, Princess (daughter of George II), 9, 180, 202.
Angellier, Auguste, 62.
Angelo, Henry, 39 n., 101 n., 102 n., 120 n., 126.
Angoulême, Duc d', 175.
Anson, George Lord, 155, 186.
Anstey, Christopher, 30.
Anville, Duc d', 153.
Apology, Churchill's, 228.
Arcadia, Lloyd's, 225.
Armentières, Marquis d', 36.
Art of Pleasing, Congreve's, 188.
Artois, Countess of, 175.
Ash, Isabella, 139, 148 149.
Assyrian Host, Destruction of the, Loutherbourg's, 124.
Athelwold, 256.
AT PRIOR PARK, 1-31.
Atterbury, Bishop, 16 n.
Auguste, the negro, 52.
Aumale, Duc d' (Henri d'Orléans), 43, 59 n.
Author's Apology, Lloyd's 216.

Bachaumont, 57.
Balguy, Dr., 26 n., 247.
Balsamo, Giuseppe, 118.
Barbarossa, Brown's, 76.
Barbier de Séville, Beaumarchais', 92.
Bard, Churchill's, 226.
Baretti, Joseph, 220, 231 n., 237.
Barré, Colonel, 51.
Barrère, 150.
Barthelémon, the violinist, 71.
Bath Postal Service, 3.
Bath Stone (oolite), 5.
Bathurst, Lord, 13.
Battle of the Nile, Loutherbourg's, 124.
Beaumarchais, Caron de, 92.
Belem, 143.
Bellecour, 91.
Beller, Liennard, the Suisse, 52.
Bensley, 218.
Berchem, Nicolas, 97.
Bernay, Mlle. de, 53.
Berry, Miss, 6, 35.
Besenval, Baron de, 60.
Bessborough House, 218.
Bessborough, Lord, 202.
Bickerton, Sir Richard, 173.
BIOGRAPHER, GRAY'S, 243-274.
Binyon, Mr. Laurence, 123.
Blanche et Guiscard, Saurin's, 81.
Blount, Martha, 12, 13, 191, 192.
Boaden's Correspondence of Garrick, 62.
Boor, Richard, 134, 137.
Borra, Signor, 186, 267.
Boswell, James, 210, 244.
Boufflers, Countess de, 58 n.
Bougainville the Elder, 43 n.
Bouquetière, *La*, Boucher's, 60.
Bourbon, Duc de, 50 n.
Bourgeois, Sir Francis, 125 n.
Bourguignon, Hubert (Gravelot), 88.
Bourne, Vincent, 212, 217.
Bousk, the Suisse, 53.
Boyce, Dr., 253.
'Boy Patriots,' The, 183, 195.
Bradshaigh, Lady, 246.
Brewster, Dr. Thomas, 1.
Bridgeman, Charles, 184.
British Theatre, Bell's, 124.

Brothers, Richard, 121.
Brown, 'Capability,' 184.
Browne, Hawkins, 213.
Browning, 256 n.
Buckingham and Chandos, second Duke of, 209.
Buckingham and Chandos, third Duke of, 209.
Buffon, M. de, 57.
Burgh, Dr., 266, 271 n.
Burlât, Barbe (Mme. Loutherbourg), 98.
Burlington, Lord, 193.
Bussy, Marquis de, 173.
Bye-Posts, 4 n.
Byrom, John, 252.
Byron, Admiral, 159.
Byng, Admiral John, 156.

Cabanès, Dr., 286-7.
Cagliostro, Count de, 118, 119.
Calas, Adieux de, Chodowiecki's, 47.
Calas. Der Grosse, Chodowiecki's, 47.
Calas, La Malheureuse Famille, Carmontelle's, 60.
Camden, Lord, 85.
Camp, Linley's, 108.
Campbell, Colin, 8.
Camperdown, Battle of, Loutherbourg's, 123.
Caractacus, Mason's, 259, 261.
Capricious Lovers, Lloyd's, 240.
Carmontelle, L. C. de, 32-61, 69, 176.
CARMONTELLE, THE PORTRAITS OF, 32-61.
Carmontelle's portrait, 48.
Carnavalet, Hôtel de, 32, 44 n.
Carrogis, Louis. *See* Carmontelle.
Carrogis, Philippe, 35.
Casanova de Seingalt, Jacques, 96.
Casanova, François, 96, 97, 98 n.
Catherine of Braganza, 94, 143 n.
Chalmers, Dr., 254.
Chambers, Sir William, 237.
Champion, Fielding's, 20.
Chantilly: Les Portraits de Carmontelle, Gruyer's, 45.
Characters of Men, Pope's, 193.
Chartres, Duc de, 36, 37, 60.

Chastellux, J.-F. de, 92.
Châtelet, Marquis du, 33.
Chaucer, 248.
Chaulnes, Duchesse de, 43 n.
Chauvelin, Abbé de, 60.
Chester, Colonel J. L., 125 n.
Chesterfield, Lord, 186.
Chevreuse, Duc de, 36, 42 n., 53.
Chevreuse, Duchesse de, 53.
Child, Sir Richard, 8.
Chinese Festival, Noverre's, 77, 78.
Chit-Chat, Lloyd's, 237.
Chodowiecki's *Journey to Dantzig*, 46.
Choiseul, Duchesse de, 32, 33.
Christmas Tale, Garrick's, 103, 104.
Churchill, Charles, 19, 210, 211, 225, 226.
Churchill, Patty, 240.
Cibber's *Apology*, 224.
Cicero, Middleton's, 268.
Cillart, M. de, 170.
Clairon, Mlle., 74, 81, 89, 90.
Clandestine Marriage, The, Garrick and Colman's, 65, 66 n., 224.
Clare, Lord, 199
Clarissa, Richardson's, 246, 256.
Clarke, General, 51.
Cobham, Lady, 191, 198.
Cobham, Lord, 13 n., 182, 183, 188, 193, 208.
Cochin, C. N., 38, 71.
Coke, Lady Mary, 32, 202, 204 n.
Coleridge, Hartley, 245, 247, 255, 259, 262.
Collé, Charles, 52, 73, 90.
Collection of Poems, Dodsley's, 249, 251.
Collier, Arthur, 139.
Collier, Dr., 146.
Collier, Jane, 139.
Collier, Margaret, 139, 144, 145, 146.
Colman, George, 80, 107 n., 211, 213, 218, 222, 259.
Conclave, Churchill's, 226.
Condé, Prince de, 50.
Conference, Churchill's, 226.
Congreve, William, 181, 187.
Connoisseur, The, 213.
Contes Moraux, Marmontel's, 236, 239.

Conti, Prince de, 58 n.
Cook's monument at Stowe, 200.
Coquelin, M., 223.
Coureur de St. Cloud, 42 n.
Courthope, Mr. W. J., 257 n.
Courtney, Mr. W. P., 251.
Covent Garden Tragedy, Fielding's, 19.
Coventry, Maria, Lady, 262.
Cowper, William, 211, 212, 215, 218, 234.
Cradock, Charlotte, 1, 19.
Critic, Sheridan's, 108.
Croix, Marquise de la, 42 n.
Cromarty, Lord, 135.
Cross-posts, 4 n.
Cry, The, Fielding and Collier's, 139.
Cumberland, Richard, 211.
Cunat, M. Charles, 151, 152, 283, 284, 286, 287.
Cyder, Philips', 136 n.
Cymon, Garrick's, 103 n.

Dalston, Miss Betty, 1.
Dance, Sir Nathaniel, 83, 84.
Daniel, Mrs., 131, 132.
Dashwood, Miss Kitty, 193.
Dauphin, The (son of Louis XV), 49.
Dauphin, The (son of Louis XVI), 175.
Dauphiness, The, 50.
Davies, Thomas, 210, 227.
Dawson, Miss Eliza, 264 n.
De Arte Graphica, Du Fresnoy's, 271.
Death of Adam, Klopstock's, 239.
Deffand, Mme. du, 32, 33, 35, 52, 55.
Dehodencq, 177, 282, 283, 286, 287.
Denis, Admiral Sir Peter, 236.
Denis, Charles, 72, 236.
Denis Duval, Thackeray's, 236.
Delany, Mrs., 6 n.
Derrick, Samuel, 22, 30.
Derwentwater, James Radcliffe, Earl of, 191.
Devonshire, Duke of, 84, 85.
Deyverdun, 118.
Diable à Quatre, Sedaine's, 76 n.
Diderot, 87, 97, 99, 100.

Diderot's *Drame Sérieux*, 93.
Divine Legation of Moses, Warburton's, 15.
Doric Arch at Stowe, Princess Amelia's, 203.
Dobell, Mr. Bertram, 103.
Douglas, Home's, 246.
Du Barry, Vicomte, 92.
Duclos, C. P., 57.
Duff, Major Lachlan Gordon, 43.
Duff, Mr. Thomas Gordon, 43 n.
Dumesnil, Mlle., 81.

Edgar, King of England, 255, 256.
Edwards, Thomas, 30.
Égalité, Philip, 39, 44 n., 50.
Egmont, Comtesse d' (1), 58.
Egmont, Comtesse d' (2), 54, 58 n.
Eidophusikon, Loutherbourg's, 111-117, 277-281.
EIGHTEENTH-CENTURY STOWE, 180-209.
Elegies, Mason's, 261.
Elegy, Gray's, 254.
Elfrida, or Ælfthryth, 255.
Elfrida, Mason's, 254, 255, 256 n., 260, 261.
Enghien, Duc d', 50 n.
England and Wales, Romantic and Picturesque Scenery in, Loutherbourg's, 124, 126.
English Garden, Mason's, 266, 270.
Essai sur les Mœurs, Voltaire's, 82.
Estaing, Count d', 159, 160.
Estcourt, Dick, 189.
Estourmel, Captain d', 153.
Etanduère, M. d', 154.
Exeter, Lord, 83.
Eybelly, Marie-Jeanne, 35.

Famous Houses of Bath, Mr. J. F. Meehan's, 6 n.
Farnborough, Lord, 123 n.
Farnham, Lord, 51.
Faulkner, Thomas, 94, 126.
Favart, C., 103.
Fêtes Chinoises, Noverre's, 77.
Fielding, Allen, 27.
Fielding, Harriot, 139, 141, 145.
Fielding, Henry, 1, 2, 19, 26 n., 72 n., 83, 129.
Fielding, Henry, Miss G. M. Godden's, 1 n., 130 n.

Fielding, Mrs., 139, 144, 145.
Fielding, Sarah, 2, 28, 139.
Fielding, Sir John, 128, 130.
Fiennes, Celia, 206.
Filon, M. Augustin, 57 n.
'FIND,' A FIELDING, 128-149.
Fittler, James, 122, 124.
Fitzgerald, Mr. Percy, 62.
Florian, J. P. C. de, 51.
Fontenelle, Bernard le Bovier de, 32.
Fordhook, 135, 137 n.
Forestier, M. Masson, 57 n.
Fosse, J. B. J. de la, 47, 60.
Foucou, the sculptor, 176.
Frénilly, Mme. de, 40.
Frénilly's *Recollections*, 40, 49 n., 275.
Fuller, Thomas, 182.
Funeral, Steele's, 194 n.

Gainsborough, Thomas, 29, 116, 124.
Galissonière, Admiral de la, 156.
Galles, Captain de, 163.
Garat's *Memoirs*, 88 n.
Garric, David (of Bordeaux), 64.
Garric, Jeanne, 65.
Garrick, David, 58, 62-93, 101 n., 102, 104.
Garrick, George, 80, 83, 84.
Garrick, Mrs., 70, 72, 81.
Garrick, Noverre on, 79.
Garrick, Peter, 74.
GARRICK'S GRAND TOUR, 62-93.
Garrick's Head, Bath, 6 n.
Garrigues, The de la, 64.
Gay, John, 112.
Genlis, Mme. de, 35, 37, 38, 41, 45, 48, 49, 50, 59.
Geoffrin, Mme, 88.
Gérard, François, 176, 282.
Gibbon, Edward, 74, 81, 118, 229.
Gibbons, Grinling, 208.
Gibbs, James, 198, 202.
Glover, Richard, 195.
Godiva, Lady, 181.
Goldsmith, Oliver, 12, 74, 216, 218 n.
Goncourts, The, 55.
Gosse, Mr. Edmund, 257 n.
Gouvernante, La Chaussée's, 81.
Gramont, Duchesse de, 54.

GRAND TOUR, GARRICK'S, 62-93.
Grasse, Count de, 161.
Gravelot (Hubert Bourgignon), 90.
Graves, Rev. Richard, 23.
Gray, Thomas, 232, 243, 247, 264, 267.
GRAY'S BIOGRAPHER, 243-274.
Gray's *Odes*, 219.
Greatbach, W., 34 n.
Great Fire of London, 123 n.
Grenville, Captain Thomas, 186.
Grimm, Baron, 35, 46, 57, 58, 66, 67, 73, 86, 87, 89.
Grub Street Journal, 19.
Gruyer, F. A., 45, 53, 54.
Guibert, Comte de, 55.

Haidar Ali, 163, 164, 165, 167, 173.
Halsewell East Indiaman, Loss of, 114, 277.
Hammersmith Terrace, 94, 117.
Hammond, James, 195.
Hannay, Mr. David, 174 n.
Hastings, Warren, 212.
Hawker, Captain, 169.
Hayman, Frank, 249.
Hecuba, Delap's, 225.
Hedgcock, Dr. F. H., 63.
Heitz, Catherine Barbe, 96.
Helvétius, Mme., 32.
Helvétius, 86.
Henry Fielding, Godden's, 1 n., 130 n.
Heroic Epistle, Mason's, 270.
Hervey, Lady, 32, 246.
Hill, Dr. Birkbeck, 243.
Hill, Joseph, 218.
Hill, The Misses, 218 n.
History of England, Bowyer's, 124.
Hogarth, William, 68 n., 95, 106, 149, 210.
Hogarth's Election Series, 46 n., 82.
Hours of the Day, Loutherbourg's, 97.
Holbach, Baron d', 57, 87, 92.
Holder, Elizabeth (Mrs. Allen), 5, 13, 14.
Holderness, Earl of, 257, 263, 265.
Holland, Sir Nathaniel Dance, 83, 84.
Houdon, J. A., 287.
Houel, 60.

Howard, Lady Ann, 202, 204 n.
Howe, Richard, Earl, 150.
Howe's Victory (June 1, 1794), 122.
Hubert of Geneva, 32.
Huchon, M. Réné, 63.
Hughes, Admiral Sir Edward, 52, 163-174.
Hume, David, 43 n., 88.
Humphry Clinker, Smollett's, 136 n.
Hunter, William, 134, 137.
Hurd, Richard, 26 n., 247, 262, 265.

Il Bellicoso, Mason's, 247.
Iliad, Pope's, 20, 22.
Il Pacifico, Mason's, 247.
Impey, Elijah, 212.
Independence, Churchill's, 240.
Installation Ode, Mason's, 253.
Irving, Sir Henry, 107.
Isis, Mason's, 252.

Jal, M. Auguste, 35, 40, 177, 178 n., 282-4, 286-7.
Jealous Wife, Colman's, 225.
Johnson, Dr., 210, 221, 243.
Johnstone, Governor James, 160, 161, 162.
Joly, M., 41.
Jones, Richard, 8.
Joseph Andrews, Fielding's, 20.
Journal Étranger, Fréron's, 75.
Journal of a Voyage to Lisbon, Fielding's, 129, 130 n., 132, 136, 139.
Journey from this World to the Next, Fielding's, 21.
Junqueira, 143.

Kemble, John, 106 n.
Kenrick, Dr., 85.
Kent, William, 185, 186, 208.
King, Commodore, 167 n., 174.
Kinloss, The Baroness, 209.
Knight, Joseph, 62.

Lacour-Gayet, M., 286.
Lacy, 80, 104.
Lafayette, 44 n.
Laitière de Villers-Cotterets, 43 n.
Lamballe, Princesse de, 51.
Lamoignon, Presidente, 54.

Langton, Bennet, 110.
Lauzun, Duchesse de, 54, 58 n.
Leake, James, 30.
Lédans, Chevalier de, 42, 58 n.
Le Kain, 91.
Le Moyne, J. B., 88.
Leofric, Earl, 181.
Leonidas, Glover's, 196.
Leroy, Dr., 286-7.
Lespinasse, Mlle. de, 55.
Lethe, Garrick's, 215.
Lettres sur les Arts imitateurs, Noverre's, 79.
Lewesden Hill, Crowe's, 114.
Lewis, Sir George, 72.
Library, Kippis's, 231.
Lilliput Alley, Bath, 5.
Linnæus, 6 n.
Lloyd, Dr. Pierson, 211, 226.
Lloyd, Robert, 66 n., 72, 259.
LLOYD, ROBERT, 210-242.
London and Wise, 184.
Londres, Grosley's, 201 n.
Long, Dr., of Pembroke Hall, 252.
Loutherbourg, Lucy de, 120, 125.
Loutherbourg, Philip de, 71, 150.
LOUTHERBOURG, R.A., 94-127.
Loutherbourg, Salome de, 125.
Lucas, Captain J. J. E., 176 n.
Louis XVI, 175.
Lying Valet, Garrick's, 76.
Lyttelton, Lord, 24, 181, 187, 196, 250, 263.

Macaulay, Lord, 243.
Mackenzie, George, Lord Cromarty, 135 n., 137.
Macklin's *Bible*, 124.
Mahan, Admiral, 172 n., 178.
Maid of the Oaks, Burgoyne's, 107.
Mainauduc, Dr. de, 118.
Marie Antoinette, 175.
Marigny, Marquis de, 57.
Marlborough, Sarah, Duchess of, 190.
Marmontel, 87, 89.
Mar's Hill (Mount Beacon), Bath, 7.
Mason, Mrs., 263.
Mason, William, 32, 234 n., 243-274.

Matthews, Admiral, 152.
Maurepas, Count de, 153.
Medland, Thomas, 206.
Meehan, Mr. J. F., 6 n.
Mémoires Secrets, Buchaumont's, 81.
Memoirs and Writings of Gray, Mason's, 243, 268.
Mesmer, F. A., 118.
Mesangère, Pierre de la, 42, 43.
Middleton, Mrs., 202.
Miger, 60.
Millar, Andrew, 134, 137, 145.
Miller, Sanderson, 267.
Milton, John, 248.
Milton miniature, Cooper's pretended, 271.
Mineral Water Hospital, Bath, 7, 14.
Minor, Foote's, 78.
Minor Poems, Milton's, 249.
Mirepoix, Prince de, 177, 283.
Mitford, John, 272.
Mitford, Miss, 270.
Miscellanies, Fielding's, 21, 22.
Monceau, Park of, 43 n., 60.
Monkhouse, Cosmo, 127 n.
Monnet, Jean, 69, 91, 101.
Monro, Dr., 116 n.
Montesson, Mme. de, 50.
Moody, Dr. Christopher Lake, 125.
More, Hannah, 118.
Morellet, Abbé, 87.
Mossop, H., 227.
Mountain, Mrs., 95.
Mount-scoundrel, 239.
Mozart, 57.
Mozart, Leopold, 57.
'Mr. Allworthy.' *See* Allen
Mr. Pope, George Paston's, 10 n.
Munby, Arthur J., 263 n.
Munro, Sir Hector, 164.
Murphy, Arthur, 62, 89.

Naish, Mr. R. G., 23 n.
Napoleon, 150.
Narcisse, the negro, 52.
Nash, Richard, 6 n.
Naumachia, The, 44 n., 60 n.
Neville, Mr., 89.
Newcastle, Duke of (Thomas Pelham Holles), 253, 262.
Night, Churchill's, 230.
Ninette à la Cour, Favart's, 240.
Nivernais, Duke de, 30.

Nollekens, Joseph, 84, 185.
Nonsense Club, The, 218, 219, 222.
Nourse, John, 129.
Nouvelle École des Femmes, de Moissy's, 236.
Nouvelles Promenades dans Paris, Cain's, 44 n.
Noverre, Jean Georges, 75.
Nugent, Mary, Marchioness of Buckingham, 199.
Nuneham, Lord, 258.

Oberkirch, Mme. d', 50.
Odes, Gray's, 259.
Odes, Mason's, 258.
Ode to a Water Nymph, Mason's, 249, 250, 251, 263.
Ode to Memory, Mason's, 220.
Ode to Obscurity, 220.
Oldfield, Mrs., 194.
Olivier's *Thé à l'Anglaise*, 57 n.
Omai, O'Keeffe's, 108.
Ombres Chinoises, 38.
O'Mélan, Abbé, 52.
Orford, Lady, 83.
Oriental Gardening, Dissertation on, Chambers's, 221.
Orléans, Louis - Philippe, Duc d', 36, 39, 50, 52, 58, 60.
Orléans, Louis-Philippe Joseph, Duc d', 37, 39, 50.
Orléans, Thérèse-Bathilde d' ('Mademoiselle'), 50.
Our Village, Miss Mitford's, 218 n.

Palladian Bridge (Prior Park), 8, 9.
Palladian Bridge (Stowe), 8, 200.
Palmerston, Lord, 83.
Paradoxe sur le Comédien, Diderot's, 69 n.
Paris, Comte de, 209.
Parlour Window, Mangin's, 106 n.
Parnasse Anglois, Patu's projected, 75.
Pascet, the enameller, 101.
Pasquin, Fielding's, 19, 238 n.
Patagonian Theatre, Dibdin and Stoppelaer's, 112.
Patu, Claude-Pierre, 75-77.
Penthièvre, Duc de, 51.
Philosophe sans le Savoir, Sedaine's, 92.
Pinero, Sir Arthur, 260.

Pitt, 28, 183, 186, 197.
Place, De la, 72 n., 73 n., 92.
Plain Truth, Fielding's, 1.
Poems, Lloyd's, 231.
Poet, Lloyd's, 228.
Polignac, Comtesse de, 54.
Pollock, Mr. Walter Herries, 69 n.
Pons-Saint-Maurice, M. de, 36.
Pont-de-Veyle, M., 52, 58 n.
Pope, Alexander, 9-15, 191, 248.
Pope's *Letters*, 10.
Powell, Dr., 247, 252.
Powys, Mrs. Lybbe, 201, 207.
Pratt, Mrs. Mary, 119, 121, 126.
Préville, 66, 68, 81.
Prior, Matthew, 213.
PRIOR PARK, AT, 1-31.
Pritchard, Miss, 75.
Pritchard, Mrs., 75, 106, 227.
Prologues, Lloyd's, 225.
Prophétie Accomplie, La, 90.
Progress of Envy, Lloyd's, 212.
Pyne, W. H., 106 n., 115, 277.

Quin, James, 18.

Racine, Louis, 57.
Ralph, James, 211.
Rambler, Johnson's, 238.
Rameau, J. P., 57, 60.
Reynolds, Captain, 167 n.
Reynolds, Sir Joshua, 116, 271.
Riccoboni, Mme., 87.
Richardson, Samuel, 2, 29, 149.
Richelieu, Marshal, 155.
Rich, John, 70.
Robinson Crusoe, Sheridan's, 108.
ROBERT LLOYD, 210-242.
Rogers, Samuel, 270.
Rosciad, Churchill's, 225.
Rostand, M. Edmond, 248.
Round, Mr. J. H., 138 n.
Routh, Martin, 251.
Ruffhead's *Pope*, 193 n.
Rumain, Comtesse de, 54.

Saint-Aubin, Auguste de, 60.
St. James's Magazine, The, 211, 232, 237.
St. Lambert, 87.
Sainte Palaye, La Curne de, 52.

'Sally Lun,' 5 n.
Salm, Princesse de, 43.
Samaritan, Mason's, 271.
Sarrazin, Jean, 65.
Savage, Richard, 11, 239.
Secular Ode, Mason's, 272.
Selima and Azor, Collier's, 107.
Séran, Comtesse de, 54.
Séraphin, Joseph François, 38.
Serres, Dominic, 170 n.
Servandoni, 105.
Sévigné, Mme. de, 32, 194 n.
Shakespeare Illustrated, Lenox's, 76.
Shakespeare in France, 73 n.
Sharp, William, 121.
Shenstone, William, 235 n.
Sheridan, R. B., 108, 224.
Sherman, Miss Mary (Mrs. Mason), 263, 264 n.
Side Lights on the Georgian Period, Paston's, 264 n.
Sidney, Sir Philip, 274.
Skroddles' (Mason), 254.
Slater, Joseph, 186.
Smart, Christopher, 234.
Smith, Adam, 88, 222.
Smith, Mr. W. M., 34 n.
Soane, Sir John, 125.
Southey, Robert, 221, 265.
Spanish Armada, Defeat of, Loutherbourg's, 123 n.
Speed, Henrietta Jane, 191.
Spencer, Lord and Lady, 83.
Spence's *Anecdotes*, 15 n.
Spenser, Edmund, 248.
Spleen, Colman's, 107.
Stage Costume, 106 n.
Stances à la Malibran, de Musset's, 225.
Stapfer, Paul, 63.
Sterne, Lawrence, 29, 58, 67 n., 80, 81.
Steyne, Lord, 190 n.
Stowe Catalogue, Forster's, 209 n.
STOWE, EIGHTEENTH-CENTURY, 180-209.
Stowe, Seeley's, 208 n.
Straus, Mr. Ralph, 249.
Stubbs, John, 140, 142.
Suard, 89, 92.
Suffolk, Lady, 13 n., 191.
Suffren, Paul de, 152.
Suffren, Pierre André, 52, 150-179, 282-287.
SUFFREN, THE BAILLI DE, 150-179.
Sultan, Bickerstaffe's, 107.

Sunk Fence, The, 184.
Swift, Jonathan, 189.
Swift on Blenheim, 207.

Tableau Mouvant, 39 n.
Talleyrand, M. de, 42, 43 n.
Tancred and Sigismunda, Thomson's, 81.
Tartre, Mme. du, 53.
Tar-Water, 82, 130.
Tears and Triumph of Parnassus, Lloyd's, 225.
Temple, Anna Chamber, Countess, 204 n., 205.
Temple, Countess, 182, 199.
Temple, Earl, 180, 204 n.
Temple, George, 199.
Temple, George, Marquess of Buckingham, 199, 207, 208.
Temple, Hester (Pitt's wife), 199.
Temple, Richard, Earl, 199.
Temple, Sir Peter, 182.
Temple, Sir Richard (1), 182.
Temple, Sir Richard (2), 182, 184, 189.
Temple, Sir Thomas, 181.
Temples of Stowe, The, 181.
Théâtre Anglais, Choix de Petites Pièces du, Patu's, 76.
THE BAILLI DE SUFFREN, 150-179, 282-287.
THE PORTRAITS OF CARMONTELLE, 32-61.
Thierry, M. Augustin, 61 n.
Thomson, James, 95, 196.
Thornton, Bonnell, 210, 212, 213, 218.
Tilliard, J. B., 60.
Tipu Saib, 173.
Tischbein, the Elder, 96.
Tom Jones, Fielding's, 2, 128.
Tom Jones, Receipt for, 23 n., 128.
Tom Thumb, Fielding's, 19.
Tooke, William, 230.
Torré, the pyrotechnist, 71.
Trollope, Anthony, 105.
Tronchin, 37.
Tucker, Miss Gertrude (Mrs. Warburton), 16.
Turner, J. M. W., 127.
Two Ladies of Syracuse, Theocritus', 237.

Universal Deluge, Loutherbourg's, 124.
Uzanne, M. Octave, 56.

Valenciennes, Attack on, Loutherbourg's, 122, 123 n.
Vanbrugh, Sir John, 185, 190.
Vanloo, Carle, 96.
Vauban, Comtesse de, 55.
Vaudreuil, Captain de, 154.
Veal, or Veale, Captain Richard, 130, 131, 140, 149.
Vengeur, Sinking of the, 150.
Venice Preserv'd, Otway's, 18.
Vérité dans le Vin, Collé's, 91.
Vermenoux, Mme. de, 42 n.
Vernet, Joseph, 88, 99.
Vigée-Lebrun, Mme., 88.
Villiers, Lord, 258.
Virginia, Crisp's, 66 n.
Voisenon, Abbé de, 57.
Voltaire, 56, 60, 76, 82, 86.
Voltaire's *Théâtre Classique*, 93.

Wade, Marshal, 3.
Walpole, Horace, 32, 33, 35, 88, 90, 92, 99, 109, 119, 180, 202, 210, 219, 221, 244, 254, 259, 261 n.
Walpole, Sir Robert, 183.
Wanstead House, 8.
Warburton, Bishop, 5, 14, 15-19, 221.
Warburton, Mrs., 16.
Ward, Dr., 130.
Ward, Dr. A. W., 195.
Ward, Mr. Humphry, 257 n.
Warley Camp, 110.
Warton, Joseph, 222.
Warton, Thomas, 247, 249, 252, 266.
Way to Keep Him, Murphy's, 236.
Webber, John, 109.
Welch, Saunders, 132, 133, 134, 137.
Wesley, Samuel, 217.
Weston, 104.
Wharton, Dr., of Durham, 250, 253.
Whitehead, William, 258.
Whittingham, Elizabeth (Sir John Fielding's wife), 138.
Whittingham, Mary Ann, 138.

Wilkes, John, 88, 210, 230, 239.
William, Fielding's footman, 139, 147, 149.
Wilson, Richard, 109.
Wine and Walnuts, W. H. Pyne's, 106n., 112n., 277.
Wolcot, Dr. ('Peter Pindar'), 99, 110.
Wonders of Derbyshire, 118 n.
Wood, John, 7, 9.
Wood, 'Palmyra,' 186, 262.
Wouverman, Philip, 99.
Wright, 109 n.

Yew Cottage, Bath, 2, 23.
York, Duke of, 43 n., 84, 122.
Young, William ('Parson Adams'), 235 n.

Zuccarelli, F., 95.